Business Analysis - Based

A Pocket Guide

I0068062

Other publications by Van Haren Publishing

Van Haren Publishing (VHP) specializes in titles on Best Practices, methods and standards within four domains:
- IT and IT Management
- Architecture (Enterprise and IT)
- Business Management and
- Project Management

Van Haren Publishing offers a wide collection of whitepapers, templates, free e-books, trainer materials etc. in the **Van Haren Publishing Knowledge Base**: www.vanharen.net for more details.

Van Haren Publishing is also publishing on behalf of leading organizations and companies: ASLBiSL Foundation, CA, Centre Henri Tudor, Gaming Works, IACCM, IAOP, IPMA-NL, ITSqc, NAF, Ngi, PMI-NL, PON, The Open Group, The SOX Institute.

Topics are (per domain):

IT and IT Management	Architecture (Enterprise and IT)	Project, Program and Risk Management
ABC of ICT	ArchiMate®	A4-Projectmanagement
ASL®	GEA®	DSDM/Atern
CATS CM®	Novius Architectuur Methode	ICB / NCB
CMMI®	TOGAF®	ISO 21500
COBIT®		MINCE®
e-CF	**Business Management**	M_o_R®
ISO 20000	B&IP	MSP™
ISO 27001/27002	BABOK® Guide	P3O®
ISPL	BiSL®	PMBOK® Guide
IT Service CMM	EFQM	PRINCE2®
ITIL®	eSCM	
MOF	IACCM	
MSF	ISA-95	
SABSA	ISO 9000/9001	
	OPBOK	
	SAP	
	SixSigma	
	SOX	
	SqEME®	

For the latest information on VHP publications, visit our website: www.vanharen.net.

Business Analysis

Based on *BABOK® Guide* Version 2
A Pocket Guide

Jarett Hailes

Van Haren
PUBLISHING

Colophon

Title:	Business Analysis Based on *BABOK® Guide* Version 2 – A Pocket Guide
Series:	Best Practice
Author:	Jarett Hailes
Text editor:	Steve Newton
Publisher:	Van Haren Publishing, Zaltbommel, www.vanharen.net
ISBN Hard copy:	978 90 8753 735 7
ISBN eBook:	978 90 8753 775 3
Edition:	First edition, first impression, June 2014
Layout and typesetting:	CO2 Premedia, Amersfoort – NL
Copyright:	© Van Haren Publishing, 2014

For any further enquiries about Van Haren Publishing, please send an e-mail to: info@vanharen.net

Preface

*"There is nothing so useless as doing efficiently that which should not
be done at all."*
- *Peter Drucker*

Understanding needs. Defining objectives. Prioritizing problems and
opportunities. Selecting the right solution. Ensuring what is delivered is
effective. All these activities and more rely on effective business analysis.

The profession of business analysis is rapidly changing and evolving.
As organizations realize how crucial it is to be able to successfully
manage and deliver change in order to survive and thrive in the global
economy, demand for business analysis skills will continue to increase.
To this day, people still have difficulty understanding the purpose
of business analysis and how it fits with other professions that are
involved in the same activities within organizations. In 2003 the
International Institute of Business Analysis™ (IIBA®) was formed to
define and develop standards for the profession and help business
analysis practitioners (called Business Analysts) improve their skills.

The IIBA developed *A Guide to the Business Analysis Body of Knowledge*®
(*BABOK*® *Guide*) to provide Business Analysts and other stakeholders

a comprehensive understanding of what business analysis is about and how it can be delivered to help organizations meet their objectives. Version 2 of the *BABOK® Guide* was released in 2009 and helped shift the focus on business analysis from mainly within the Information Technology domain to one that enables all aspects of the organization to improve their performance and deliver solutions to meet their needs. The *BABOK® Guide* delivers a wealth of information about business analysis, but it can be difficult to know where to start or how to apply its content. Since the profession has evolved since the release of Version 2, there are certain aspects of business analysis that are under-represented in the current version of the *BABOK® Guide*. The purpose of this pocket guide is to provide a clear, concise summary of the key ideas from the *BABOK® Guide* while also offering additional competencies (competences), techniques and ways to apply business analysis within organizations.

Current Business Analysts can use this pocket guide as a quick reference to key concepts. Other stakeholders involved in business analysis activities, from C-suite executives to project team members to front-line staff, can use this guide to gain an understanding of the value business analysis has within an organization and how to effectively interact with Business Analysts.

As you review this pocket guide, I encourage you to think about your organization's mission, goals, and objectives, as well as its current operations, and consider what its key success factors are going forward. From this starting point you can leverage the content from this pocket guide and the *BABOK® Guide* to ensure your organization focuses its energy on what truly matters and is able to successfully deliver solutions that meet its needs.

May 2014,
Jarett Hailes, CBAP

Contents

1 Introduction

1.1 Purpose of the Pocket Guide

The purpose of this pocket guide to the International Institute of Business Analysis™ (IIBA) *A Guide to the Business Analysis Body of Knowledge*® (or '*BABOK*® *Guide*' for short) is to help understand the key knowledge found within the *BABOK*® *Guide* and how it can be applied to a particular situation. This pocket guide can be used by:

■ Individuals interested in how business analysis works or who may want to become Business Analysts;

■ Business Analysts as a quick reference during the course of their day-to-day work;

■ Team members working on projects or within normal organizational operations where business analysis is performed;

■ Managers and executives who need to understand how business analysis can help improve their organizations.

This pocket guide is based upon the content found in Version 2 of the *BABOK*® *Guide*, published in 2009[1].

Throughout this guide, you will see boxes that contain information of particular interest. Each box has one of the following symbols:

Note: defines a key concept or explains it in greater detail;

Example: a sample situation or description of a particular task is performed;

Tip: ways to help apply the *BABOK® Guide* in a meaningful way.

1.2   What is Business Analysis?

Business analysis as a profession is relatively young, but the core activities that encompass its value have been performed by a wide variety of individuals within modern organizations for quite some time.

> **Note:** According to the *BABOK® Guide* "business analysis is the set of tasks and techniques used to work as a liaison among stakeholders in order to understand the structure, policies and operations of an organization, and recommend solutions that enable the organization to achieve its goals".

Fundamentally, business analysis is about:

- Understanding an organization's core goals and objectives;
- Being able to identify and assess key drivers that enable the organization to meet its goals and objectives;
- Determining how an organization's people, processes, structures and technologies work together as a system to perform their operations and how this ties to its goals and objectives;
- Defining the needs of the organization based on its key drivers, goals and objectives as well as its current capabilities and future potential;

- Evaluating potential solutions that will enable the organization to realize its goals and objectives.

As implied by the *BABOK® Guide* definition, business analysis is an **enabling** function that works with many groups of people who are involved directly and indirectly with an organization. Business analysis takes information from internal staff, customers, suppliers, partners, and vendors to develop a comprehensive understanding of the organization as it pertains to a particular problem or situation being analyzed (or the problem 'domain').

> **Note:** For the purposes of the *BABOK® Guide* and this pocket guide, a Business Analyst is an individual who performs business analysis activities, regardless of what their formal job title is.

As a result, Business Analysts need to be able to comprehend and process information that will often be conveyed from many different perspectives. To successfully perform business analysis, a Business Analyst must be able to understand information from many different industries and professions, each of which have their own set of terminology, standards, cultures and perception of the organization. Business Analysts take information from all these sources, determine what is relevant and valuable, and then use that information to define the organization's needs and assess potential solutions.

⚠️ **Example:** Many Business Analysts help Information Technology solution providers understand the needs of their client, whether it is an external organization or the other departments within their own organization. In this setting, Business Analysts often develop materials that allow both parties to agree on what is needed and how the solution will meet those needs.

1.3   The Need for Business Analysis

Most modern organizations are comprised of the following people, processes and tools:

- Executives focused on defining and achieving strategic goals and outcomes;
- Front-line staff focused on executing their assigned tasks as efficiently as possible;
- Managers focused on ensuring their teams meet or go beyond the expectations of their superiors;
- Customers focused on their experience with the product or service they receive;
- Suppliers and vendors focused on delivering what they need to in order to retain and increase their business with their client;
- An array of information technology, communication, and other systems that help facilitate processes, knowledge management, and interaction with all the above stakeholders.

Each person and group within this collection has different viewpoints, skills, backgrounds and priorities that make it difficult for them to see how to effectively utilize the organization's resources in order to solve problems and capitalize on opportunities:

- Executives may be able to see the big picture but don't have a deep understanding of the organization's capabilities to decide which components should be leveraged for a particular initiative;
- Front-line staff may not be empowered or realize how to make changes that will work towards the company's strategic objectives, or have their own vision and priorities that compete with the executive view;
- Managers are too busy putting out the daily fires to dedicate time to bridge the vision and priorities of their staff and superiors;
- Suppliers, vendors and even different departments within the same organization are conversant in the language of their domains, but may not be able to effectively interpret how other stakeholders think and talk.

These problems are only exacerbated as organizations grow and/or are forced to adapt to changes in their industries.

Business analysis takes information from all of these people, groups, and tools to assess what the true needs of the organization are and find solutions that will effectively address those needs. It allows individuals and teams to get a holistic view of all relevant information related to a particular goal and helps facilitate the assessment and implementation of solutions that will achieve that goal.

Business analysis delivers value to organizations by:

- ☑ Focusing on needs that are paramount to the goals of the organization, which helps maximize the use of scarce resources to solve what truly needs solving;
- ☑ Enabling organizations to find the right solutions as efficiently as possible;

☑ Developing a performance framework that enables ongoing measurement, assessment and improvement of critical business functions and future opportunities.

1.4   About IIBA

IIBA® was formed in 2003 in Canada by 28 founding members[2] who were dedicated to promoting the emerging profession of business analysis. The organization initially focused on the development of professional standards, certifications and a collective body of knowledge.

The organization has grown by leaps and bounds since then, and now has over 26,000 members around the world in 134 countries.

Today the organization has several key offerings that help aspiring and seasoned Business Analysts develop their skills, give employers the ability to assess and improve the performance of their Business Analysts, and build relationships with other professions and organizations to enhance the value Business Analysts can deliver. These offerings include:

- Support for chapters to develop and engage the local community of Business Analysts within a region;
- Learning opportunities through regular webinars, newsletters and best practice articles;
- Certification of education providers to deliver training that aligns with the *BABOK® Guide*;
- Special interest groups focused on the use of business analysis within a particular industry;
- Sponsorship of the multi-disciplined annual Building Business Capability conference that enables Business Analysts to gain

insights into techniques, ideas and approaches that can improve
their day-to-day activities.

Additionally, IIBA offers two levels of certification. These certifications
help organizations understand a base level of knowledge that
the certified individual possesses and provides individuals with
recognition for their experience as Business Analysts. Both of these
certifications require completion of an exam based on the *BABOK®
Guide* content:

- **Certification of Competency in Business Analysis (CCBA):** for
  Business Analysts with some experience; individuals must have
  performed at least 3,750 hours of business analysis work;
- **Certified Business Analysis Professional (CBAP):** designed to
  recognize those with an extensive depth and breadth business
  analysis experience; individuals must have performed at least 7,500
  hours of business analysis work in the past 10 years.

1.5   About the *BABOK® Guide*

The *BABOK® Guide* defines the scope of what it means to perform
business analysis and how the major concepts and tasks that make up
this profession relate to one another.

BABOK® Guide History

- January 2005 (Version 1.0): outline and key definitions;
- October 2005 (Version 1.4): draft content of some knowledge areas;
- June 2006 (Version 1.6): details for most knowledge areas;
- October 2008 (Version 1.6 errata);
- March 2009 (Version 2.0): refine, simplify, and integrate knowledge areas,
  tasks and techniques.

Within each iteration of the *BABOK® Guide*, IIBA sought community
involvement to ensure the end product was as relevant to as many

practicing Business Analysts as possible and would represent best
practices within the profession.

The *BABOK® Guide* provides a framework containing several key
elements:

- **Knowledge areas:** a collection of related tasks that form a major
  function of business analysis. The *BABOK® Guide* defines six
  knowledge areas, which are discussed in Section 1.7.
- **Tasks:** a specific type of work that is performed in order to
  accomplish a particular goal. Each task within the *BABOK® Guide*
  has a specific purpose, description, set of inputs and outputs,
  elements, relevant techniques that can be applied, and set of
  stakeholders involved.
- **Techniques:** describe a particular way that a task can be
  accomplished. Many of the techniques described within the
  BABOK® Guide are often a component of the overall work to be
  performed to complete a task, and some can be applied to multiple
  tasks.
- **Underlying competencies:** represent certain basic aptitudes that
  Business Analysts require in order to be able to effectively perform
  the tasks defined within the *BABOK® Guide*.
- **Terms:** standard definitions for common words that are used
  throughout the *BABOK® Guide*. The *BABOK® Guide's* glossary
  provides clear descriptions for all major relevant terms.

> **Note:** The *BABOK® Guide* is not prescriptive in how a Business Analyst
> should go about performing their tasks on a particular initiative.
> A methodology or specific set of procedures applies the information from
> the *BABOK® Guide* to a given situation.

1.6   Key Terms to Understand

Before reading further, it is important to understand some of the key
terms used within the *BABOK® Guide* and this pocket guide:

- **Stakeholder:** a group or individual who have interests that may be
  affected by an initiative, or who have influence over it;
- **Solution:** a set of components that meet a business need by
  solving a problem or enable an organization to capitalize on an
  opportunity;
- **Requirement:** a condition or capability needed by a stakeholder to
  solve a problem or achieve an objective;
- **Initiative:** an effort undertaken to achieve a specific goal or
  objective.

Business analysis may be performed within a project environment or
within the course of an organization's ongoing operations. The term
initiative will be used to denote the performance of business analysis
in either context.

Requirements can be further classified into the following groupings to
assist with business analysis tasks:

- **Business requirements:** high level goals or objectives of the
  organization – they define **why** an initiative is being performed;
- **Stakeholder requirements:** define **what** is needed for a particular
  stakeholder or collection of stakeholders;
- **Solution requirements:** describe characteristics of a particular
  solution that will meet business and stakeholder requirements;
- **Transition requirements:** capabilities which the solution needs
  to move the organization from its current state to the future state
  when the solution is implemented, but are not needed after the
  transition is completed.

> **Note:** Solution requirements can be further classified as either
> **functional requirements** that describe the behavior of the solution or
> **non-functional requirements** that define environmental conditions that
> regulate how the solution should operate.

Unless otherwise noted, this pocket guide uses the *BABOK® Guide*
definition for all terms within its text.

1.7   Knowledge Areas, Techniques and Their Inter-Relationships

As mentioned above, there are six knowledge areas within the
BABOK® Guide:

- **Business Analysis Planning and Monitoring:** governs how all
  other business analysis tasks are performed;
- **Elicitation:** how to identify and understand requirements;
- **Requirements Management and Communication:** describes
  how to structure, organize and communicate requirements to
  stakeholders;
- **Enterprise Analysis:** defines how to define business requirements
  and assess whether a particular problem is worthy of further effort
  in order to solve it;
- **Requirements Analysis:** discusses how to assess requirements in
  order to understand what is needed to solve a problem or capitalize
  on an opportunity;
- **Solution Assessment and Validation:** describes how to assess
  current and potential solutions and address any shortcomings, and
  to facilitate the transition to a new solution.

Knowledge areas describe a collection of related tasks, however these
tasks may not necessarily be performed in sequence, nor are the
knowledge areas performed in a particular order. Each task has a set
of inputs and outputs that could come from any other knowledge area.
See figure 1.1.

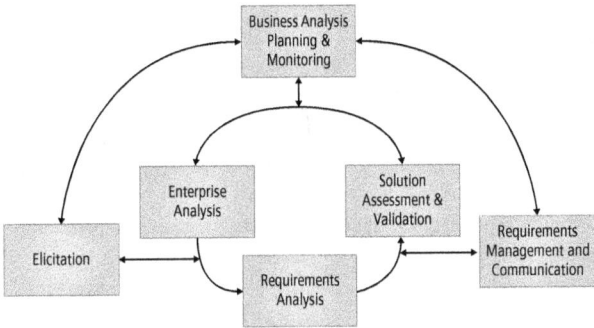

Figure 1.1 Knowledge areas and their inter-relationships

In addition to the knowledge areas, the *BABOK® Guide* contains a set of techniques that can be applied in a variety of tasks. Techniques support the performance of tasks but may not be the only actions that need to be performed to complete a task. A set of general techniques are defined in Chapter 9 of the *BABOK® Guide*; some tasks also describe other techniques not found in Chapter 9 but which are relevant to that task.

1.8 Stakeholders and Their Influence on Business Analysis

There are three main types of stakeholders who are involved in a particular initiative:

■ Team members involved in accomplishing the initiative with the Business Analyst. Potential team members include implementation subject matter experts, managers, testers, and other Business Analysts;

■ Stakeholders who are directly affected by the results of the initiative, such as end users and sponsors;

■ Stakeholders who are indirectly affected by the results of the initiative.

> **Note:** Stakeholders such as customers, suppliers, and regulators may be directly or indirectly affected by a particular initiative, depending on the particular context of the situation.

The particular makeup of the stakeholders involved in an initiative will greatly influence how business analysis is performed. Certain techniques may not be feasible while others may be explicitly denied. Some key factors include:

☑ Where are stakeholders located and how can they be engaged in specific tasks?

☑ What are the attitudes, influences and levels of engagement within each stakeholder group in relation to the initiative?

☑ How do the various stakeholder groups feel about one another and are there potential issues which could arise when performing specific tasks that involve multiple groups?

☑ Are there any particular cultural differences that would preclude or alter how certain tasks will be performed?

☑ Do any of the stakeholders have specific expectations or mandatory approaches or methods that must be used when performing business analysis?

> **Example:** Representatives from one stakeholder group often dominate workshops, presenting their point of view. Instead of performing a workshop, the Business Analyst decides it is more appropriate to perform interviews with each stakeholder group individually.

Section 2.2 discusses stakeholder analysis and how its outputs are used throughout other business analysis tasks.

2 Business Analysis Planning and Monitoring

To effectively perform business analysis you need to plan how the business analysis activities will be executed and understand how to assess the value of the outputs from those activities. The plan should be based on the context of:

- What you are trying to accomplish and the reasons why it is worthwhile;
- Your organizational environment;
- What assets and tools you have available at your disposal.

There are six Business Analysis Planning and Monitoring tasks:

1. **Plan business analysis approach:** determine how the overall business analysis work will be completed.
2. **Conduct stakeholder analysis:** identify and classify people and groups who are affected by the project or initiative.
3. **Plan business analysis activities:** define which specific business activities will be performed, the outputs that will be generated, and the amount of time and effort required to perform the activities.
4. **Plan business analysis communication:** describe how business analysis activities and outputs will be communicated, to whom, and when.

5. **Plan requirements management process:** determine how requirements and the scope of the solution will be managed as changes occur over time.
6. **Manage business analysis performance:** identify how the performance of business analysis activities will be assessed and improved.

The resulting plans and associated documents produced during these tasks are used to guide and monitor all of the other activities that Business Analysts perform in the context of a particular project or initiative.

2.1   Plan Business Analysis Approach

An approach to performing business analysis activities is used to govern the development of specific business analysis plans. Organizations may define a formal, repeatable approach (called a method) to ensure consistency between various projects or initiatives.

> **Note:** The approach describes the characteristics of how activities should be performed, while the plan defines the details of the activities for the particular effort being undertaken.

The business analysis approach should address the following questions:
- ☑ When are business analysis activities being performed in the context of the other activities of the project or initiative?
- ☑ What format and structure will business analysis deliverables take?
- ☑ How will requirements be prioritized?
- ☑ How will changes to requirements be managed?
- ☑ How will the detailed business analysis plan be developed?
- ☑ What types of communication will be used with stakeholders?
- ☑ What tools will be used to manage and analyze requirements?

There are two general types of approaches taken to perform business analysis activities. Most approaches fall somewhere between these two extremes:

■ **Plan-driven approaches** often have very structured stages with formal controls placed on proceeding between each stage. Plan-driven approaches focus on identifying as many requirements as possible initially, and serve as the basis for determining subsequent stages of the initiative.

■ **Change-driven approaches** focus on iteratively producing tangible results that solve a portion of the business need. Requirements outside of the current iteration are often left at a high level and are not subject to strict change control processes.

If there is no prescribed approach for the effort being undertaken, or there are parts of the approach that must be customized for the particular effort, the Business Analyst takes into account the following considerations:

■ The business need being addressed and the nature of the initiative to address the business need;

■ The organizational process assets available, such as methodologies, defined business analysis processes, tools and templates;

■ Internal or external expertise available from Business Analysts or Business Analyst groups.

⚠ **Example:** The approach taken to determine the requirements to implement a new enterprise-wide information system will likely be very different to the approach for assessing a request to modify a screen on an existing software solution, given the difference in complexity and breadth of the impact of each effort.

2.2   Conduct Stakeholder Analysis

Whenever an effort is undertaken, there is at least one individual or group who is affected by the end result. Business Analysts need to know who these people are and how they need to be engaged in order to successfully achieve the effort's objectives.

Stakeholder analysis helps answer the following questions:
- ☑ Who is directly or indirectly affected by the initiative?
- ☑ What are the relevant characteristics of each stakeholder that pertain to the initiative?
- ☑ What are the commonalities amongst stakeholders and how can they be grouped?
- ☑ Which stakeholders need to be involved in specific business analysis activities and in what capacity?

> **Tip:** Stakeholder analysis is not only needed for business analysis activities. In projects this task is often performed in collaboration with the Project Manager and/or Change Management staff, as they also require detailed information on the groups affected by the project's end product.

Stakeholders may be categorized in several different ways:
- Organization or organizational unit;
- Job function;
- Hierarchical level (e.g. executives, supervisors, front-line staff);
- Domain knowledge/skillset;
- Some other common characteristic (e.g. an end user of the information system).

Each stakeholder group should share common characteristics that are relevant to the initiative. Some of the potential characteristics captured for each stakeholder group include:

- Their overall role in the initiative;
- Key contacts within the group and their respective roles;
- Relevant metrics about the group (e.g. number of people or organizations, revenue or cost information);
- Their attitude, influence, and level of engagement in the effort;
- Their authority for particular business analysis deliverables (e.g. approval, review, consult, end consumer);
- Risks and opportunities that could affect the outcome of the initiative.

The resulting stakeholder matrix is used to determine what specific business analysis activities are required.

Tip: This matrix should be updated continuously as the effort undertaken progresses to ensure activities are adapted if there is a change in a stakeholder's role or attitude towards the effort.

2.3 Plan Business Analysis Activities

The business analysis plan is the central component guiding other Business Analyst activities. See figure 2.1. The content and format of the plan can vary due to several factors:

- Desired outcomes from the initiative;
- Complexity of the initiative;
- Approach taken to address the business need;
- Organizational or environmental norms or standards that must be met.

When developing a business analysis plan, the Business Analyst is applying the approach they have defined in Section 2.1. While the approach describes how to go about getting the work done, the plan specifies exactly what activities will be performed, how much effort

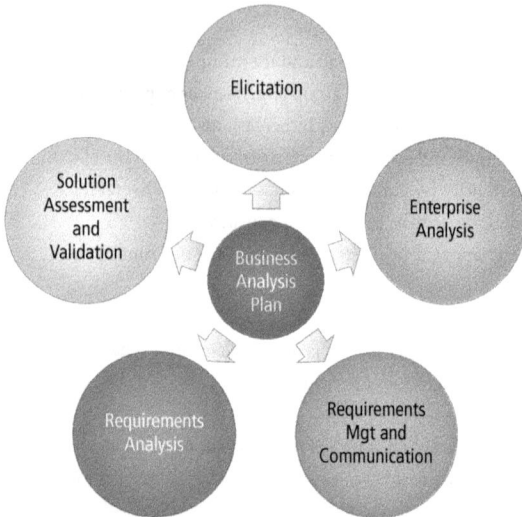

Figure 2.1 The business analysis plan is used by all other knowledge areas

they will take and their relationships to each other and non-business analysis activities.

Building the business analysis plan can involve working back from the end result to identify the necessary activities:

1. **Assess target outcomes:** what needs to have occurred when the business analysis activities are completed?
2. **Identify deliverables:** in order to meet your outcomes, what work products are needed?
3. **Determine activities:** what actions need to occur in order to produce the required deliverables?
4. **Define activity relationships:** which activities have dependencies with one another or external events or actions?

5. **Estimate effort and duration:** how much time will it take to complete each activity, both in terms of hours spent on a task and total time elapsed from the beginning of the activity until it is finished?

> **Tip:** When identifying the activities needed to complete a deliverable, consider the stakeholders involved and the process that will be used to approve and finalize the document.

The plan should not be viewed as a set-in-stone design that will absolutely yield the desired outcome. As you implement the plan and receive feedback or new information, the plan can and should adapt as required. A description of how to adapt the plan should be incorporated into the plan itself.

2.4   Plan Business Analysis Communication

With a business analysis plan in place, you are now ready to go out and start doing real work, right? Not so fast. Before you engage your stakeholders in earnest, you need to plan how you will communicate with them.

> **Tip:** Communication plans often only consider the information being transmitted by the team to their stakeholders. But it is just as important to cover off how information will be received and handled, both during planned activities and on an ad-hoc basis. When building your communication plan, consider both aspects.

While the business analysis plan identified communication activities and their relationships to other business analysis activities, the communications plan goes a step further and defines:

☑ **What needs to be communicated:** for example requirements or other deliverables, notices of upcoming activities that require involvement, or general background information;

☑ **Who receives the communication:** the type of stakeholders who will receive the communication should be taken into account when defining the other aspects of the communication;

☑ **When the communication will occur:** including its frequency if appropriate;

☑ **How the information will be communicated:** which describes the format, formality, communication medium (written or oral), and distribution method.

If you also incorporate managing incoming communications into your plan, you should specify:

■ What inbound communication mechanisms will be established (e.g. surveys, dedicated e-mail account or phone line, regular town hall meetings);

■ How ad-hoc communications received will be processed, in particular how information that impacts requirements or deliverables will be dealt with;

■ How inbound communications will be logged and tracked as they are processed.

> **Note:** The business analysis communication plan is developed in the context of the business analysis activities that need to be performed. If there is an overall communication plan for the initiative, the business analysis communication plan should integrate into the overall communication plan.

The business analysis communication plan drives how deliverables are structured and presented to stakeholders, in particular requirements packages (see Section 4.4 for more information).

2.5   Plan Requirements Management Process

Requirements are what are used to determine how to solve the problem
at hand. As a result, you need to ensure the requirements are handled
in a way that will allow you to ensure they are adequately reviewed and
approved, and can adapt to changing information or circumstances.
There are five main considerations to the requirements management
process:

1. What requirement attributes will be captured?
2. How and where will requirements be stored?
3. Will requirements be traced between one another and with other
   elements, such as test cases or solution specifications? If so, how
   will this be done?
4. How will requirements be prioritized?
5. When new requirements are uncovered or existing requirements
   change, how will proposed changes be managed?

> **Tip:** The business analysis approach may sufficiently address
> requirements management questions. If not, it is worthwhile to
> document their processes separately.

As with the overall business analysis plan and communication plan,
the answers to these questions depends on the initiative you are
undertaking, the stakeholders involved, and the environment you are
working in.

2.6   Manage Business Analysis Performance

Business analysis activities themselves can be measured and assessed
to determine if there are ways in which they can be improved. In
order to improve the performance of a Business Analyst, you need the
following information:

☑ A set of performance measures that can provide meaningful
   insight into the activities performed by the Business Analyst;

☑ An understanding of what the Business Analyst is expected to do, which is typically represented by the business analysis plan.

Examples of performance measures that can be relevant to a Business Analyst's work include:

- The variances from estimated deliverable completion dates and actual completion dates, or from estimated to actual effort required;
- The number of changes to requirements that occur after approval or finalization of requirements;
- Stakeholder or manager assessments of the quality of the deliverables created by the Business Analyst;
- Satisfaction scores for the activities led or performed by the Business Analyst.

Example: Events facilitated by a Business Analyst, such as a requirements workshop, structured walkthrough, or information session, are good opportunities to receive feedback on the Business Analyst's performance through feedback forms or brief surveys.

Once a Business Analyst's performance has been measured, the information can be assessed and reported to the Business Analyst, their superiors and other stakeholders. Opportunities for improvement can be identified and support can be provided to correct any issues that arise.

Tip: Sometimes poor results are not simply due to the person performing the activities. There may be issues with the plan, approach, tools or techniques that the Business Analyst was required to use and follow. Root cause analysis can help identify potential issues in the organizational process assets currently in place.

3 Elicitation

Successfully eliciting requirements is the key to ensuring a solution meets the true needs of stakeholders. Business Analysts do not 'gather' requirements; gathering implies that the requirements are readily apparent and can be easily identified and documented. Eliciting requirements means the Business Analyst has to go deeper and bring out the true requirements that will determine what kind of solution is needed.

> **Tip:** While specific activities are performed to formally elicit requirements, new or changed requirements may be elicited throughout other Business Analysis activities.

Elicitation activities follow a simple linear path involving four tasks: prepare for elicitation, conduct elicitation, document elicitation results and confirm elicitation results. See figure 3.1.

3.1 Prepare for Elicitation

To prepare for an elicitation activity you need to:

- ☑ Review the scope you are attempting to elicit requirements for;
- ☑ Assess who will be involved in the elicitation activity;

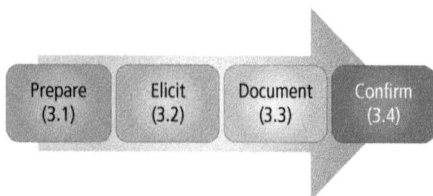

Figure 3.1 Elicitation process

☑ Determine the type of elicitation technique(s) to use for the
  activity;
☑ Plan how to perform the elicitation activity;
☑ Prepare any materials needed and obtain other resources that will
  be used, such as facilities or equipment;
☑ Communicate with stakeholders who will be involved in the
  elicitation activity and schedule an appropriate time to perform the
  activity.

The type of elicitation activity you perform should be based on the
business need, the solution scope and the stakeholders that will be
involved.

Tip: Not all elicitation activities involve engaging stakeholders directly.
You may review existing documents or other organizational assets to
elicit some requirements.

3.2   Conduct Elicitation Activity

Once you've prepared for your elicitation activity, you are ready to
perform the elicitation. There are many techniques that can be used to
elicit requirements:

- **Requirements workshops:** sessions dedicated to eliciting requirements. These sessions are structured to bring together a group of stakeholders and identify, assess, and prioritize requirements.
- **Focus groups:** bring together a group of individuals who represent a sample of certain stakeholder groups and get their views on a certain topic. Generally focus group responses are collected into high-level themes and statements instead of specific details.
- **Interviews:** an interactive session with one or more people where the interviewer asks questions to the interviewees. Interviews usually involve a set of pre-determined questions, although in some cases the interviewer may wish to have an unstructured interview with no prepared questions.
- **Brainstorming:** attempting to come up with as many possible ideas around a specific topic or problem. Brainstorming may be performed as part of a requirements workshop, focus group or interview, or it can be an activity undertaken by a single individual on their own.
- **Prototyping:** developing a functioning or non-functioning sample of the solution to provide insight into the interface of the solution and/or determine specific details of how the solution is expected to behave.
- **Observation:** watching stakeholders do their work in their regular environment to elicit requirements, either passively or by actively discussing with the observed person while they are doing the work.
- **Survey/questionnaire:** asking questions to an audience, who often reply in writing. Surveys are typically used to get information from a large group of stakeholders who otherwise would not be able to participate in the requirements elicitation process.

- **Document analysis:** review existing documentation and find requirements that pertain to the initiative. Document analysis is particularly useful when working on a multi-phase project. The Business Analyst must consider how current and correct the information found within the document is, since some information may not be up-to-date or valid.
- **Interface analysis:** reviewing or assessing interfaces between components of a solution. This could be a user interface with an information system, a person-to-person interface that occurs in a process, or a system-to-system interface. Interface analysis is especially helpful when looking for details around the input/output information required in a process or component of a solution.

> **Tip:** When performing elicitation activities with groups, it is helpful to ensure everyone understands the terminology used in the conversation. Have a glossary of terms available for participants to clarify any confusion that may arise.

Once you have completed your elicitation, you have a raw set of information that you have collected during the activity. The next step is to structure this information into a form appropriate for use in further business analysis activities.

3.3   Document Elicitation Results

When documenting elicitation results, information that is typically unstructured or unrefined (such as notes, photos, whiteboard drawings, videos and the like) are put in a format that allows them to be used by the Business Analyst in future activities. There are three main types of information that are typically documented:

- Requirements are placed in a format that is appropriate given the business analysis approach being adopted (for example, user stories written on cards or detailed requirement statements in a requirements management tool);
- Stakeholder concerns that were identified during the elicitation activity;
- Assumptions or possible constraints that were identified and require verification. These assumptions and constraints should be traced to the requirements they affect, so these requirements can be reviewed once the assumptions and constraints are verified.

> **Note:** In formal projects, stakeholder concerns are typically placed into issue and/or risk logs that are managed by the Project Manager.

Once the elicited requirements are documented, they are only considered to be 'stated'. Until these requirements, as documented, have been confirmed with the stakeholders who were involved in the elicitation session, they should not be used in subsequent tasks.

3.4   Confirm Elicitation Results

Unconfirmed requirements (and any associated stakeholder concerns, assumptions and constraints) represent the Business Analyst's interpretation of the information that has been elicited. Once this information has been documented, it is usually appropriate to go back to the stakeholders who were involved in the elicitation activity and ensure they feel the documentation accurately reflects their requirements.

Once requirements are confirmed, they can be used in subsequent tasks such as:

- Defining the business need for an initiative;
- Specifying and modeling requirements to provide stakeholders with an overview of a set of requirements;
- Prioritizing requirements;
- Defining transition requirements that are needed as part of the implementation of a solution but are no longer needed once a solution is in place.

4 Requirements Management and Communication

At various stages of an initiative, requirements need to be organized, structured, presented and approved. This knowledge area deals with managing requirements throughout their lifecycle and ensuring they are properly communicated to stakeholder audiences. There are five Requirements Management and Communication tasks:

1. **Manage solution scope and requirements:** get requirements approved within the context of the scope of the solution.
2. **Manage requirements traceability:** track the relationships between requirements and other relevant items, as well as with other requirements.
3. **Maintain requirements for re-use:** put requirements in a form that can be used by the organization after the completion of the initiative.
4. **Prepare requirements package:** structure requirements in a way that they can be understood by stakeholders in order to provide feedback and/or approve.
5. **Communicate requirements:** present requirements to stakeholders.

4.1   Manage Solution Scope and Requirements

Requirements often need some form of approval before they are used by others to perform activities such as designing, developing, assessing, or purchasing a solution. The formality of the approval process will vary depending on the scale, scope and approach taken for an initiative and the current stage in the initiative.

> **Note:** The stakeholder roles and responsibilities determined in Section 2.2 are needed in this task to ensure the proper individuals are involved in the approval of requirements.

When preparing requirements for approval, consider the following:

- ☑ How do the requirements match the scope of the solution? If there are requirements that are out of scope, part of the approval process may involve determining whether these requirements should be removed or whether the scope should be changed;

- ☑ How will disagreements over requirements be resolved? If conflicting requirements have been elicited from different stakeholders, or groups cannot agree on whether certain requirements are in scope or not, the Business Analyst should determine how to resolve these situations;

- ☑ How will the review process work? Consider how many review cycles are needed, if there are dependencies within the approval process and how feedback will be incorporated prior to subsequent stages of the process;

- ☑ How will requirements be presented? This includes consideration for both the format of the requirements and the delivery mechanism (for example, a group session versus sending out a document to be reviewed individually);

- ☑ How will feedback received during the process and final approvals be documented?

Tip: For some initiatives it may be appropriate to present subsets of
requirements to stakeholders who have authority for a component of the
overall solution scope for approval instead of presenting all requirements to
all stakeholders.

4.2   Manage Requirements Traceability

Tracing requirements involves identifying relationships between
requirements and other items. Some of the typical items that are
traced to requirements include:

- Business goals and objectives;
- Organizational units or roles;
- Solution components;
- Test cases;
- Other requirements;
- Business rules;
- Risks and issues.

Note: Requirements can be traced at an individual or aggregate level.

Tracing gives you the ability to perform many activities that support
the development of a solution:

- **Requirements analysis:** assess how detailed requirements tie
  in to high-level requirements, how stakeholder and solution
  requirements meet business requirements, evaluate solution scope
  and prioritize requirements;
- **Solution assessment:** determine which solution components
  address particular requirements, and if there are any gaps between
  the solution's capabilities and the requirements;
- **Solution testing and validation:** ensure the solution delivers the
  promised functionality by assessing whether the test cases built for
  the solution cover all requirements;

- **Solution change management:** assess the impact of a potential change to the requirements or to the solution;
- **Organizational change management:** assess how requirements being met/not met will affect the people within an organization;
- **Risk and issue management:** track which requirements have related issues and risks associated to them;
- **Requirements communication:** determine which requirements need to be communicated to particular stakeholders.

Requirement/Test Case	T-001	T-002	T-003	T-004	T-005	T-006
R-001	X					
R-002	X					
R-003	X					
R-004		X		X	X	
R-005			X			
R-006			X			
R-007			X			
R-008		X				X
R-009						X
R-010						X
R-011					X	
R-012				X	X	
R-013			X			

Figure 4.1 Example of traceability matrix between test cases and requirements

Attributes can be added to inter-requirement relationships to support these activities:

- **Necessity:** in order to meet a particular requirement another requirement must also be met;
- **Effort:** one requirement is easier or harder to implement when another requirement is also met;
- **Subset:** a portion of one requirement is addressed by another requirement;

- **Cover:** a set of requirements completely addresses another
  requirement;
- **Value:** the value of meeting a particular requirement goes up or
  down depending on whether another requirement is met.

4.3   Maintain Requirements for Re-Use

Requirements are often developed within the context of a particular
initiative to solve a problem. Once the initiative is completed, teams
may abandon the work product of their business analysis efforts
because a solution has been successfully implemented. This may result
in a loss of organizational knowledge that could greatly facilitate
future initiatives as well as support ongoing operations.

Maintaining requirements for re-use:
- Enables other Business Analysts and organizational staff to
  understand what was built and what problem the solution is
  solving;
- Allows for the assessment of requested changes to a solution and an
  understanding of their impact;
- Supports compliance with auditing standards, particularly in
  regulated industries or government;
- Provides future initiatives or project phases with a starting point
  for assessing requirements that are currently not met.

> **Tip:** The format and structure of reusable requirements depends on how
> the organization maintains its corporate knowledge. Potential recipients
> of reusable requirements should be made aware of how to access and
> leverage the information contained in the end product.

When documenting requirements for re-use, ensure the following
characteristics are included:

☑ Has the requirement been met by the solution that was developed by the initiative?

☑ Is the requirement an ongoing requirement that needs to be continually met beyond the completion of the initiative?

For requirements that were not met, an explanation for the reasons why they were not addressed in the initiative can help with future prioritization and value assessment activities.

⚠ **Example:** A collection of requirements were deemed out of scope for a project due to budget constraints. However, they were recognized as being a high priority item to address in the future should additional funding become available. This information can be used in future Enterprise Analysis tasks to assess business needs and develop business cases.

4.4   Prepare Requirements Package

Requirements packages are representations of a collection of requirements for consumption by stakeholders. They are structured so that the information is presented in an understandable format for the audience. The requirements package may include text, diagrams, models, or other forms of communicating information.

Some of the typical reasons for creating a requirements package include:

■ Receive feedback on requirements that have been elicited;

■ Obtain approval for a collection of requirements;

■ Use by other team members for activities such as product development, testing, business case development and solution assessment.

When preparing a requirements package, it is important to consider the following items in the context of the audience and intended use:

☑ What is the appropriate delivery mechanism: should it be a document, website, presentation or some other method?

☑ What content needs to be delivered?

☑ What format should the content be presented in?

☑ How much detail is needed?

> ⚠ **Example:** The level of detail needed when presenting requirements for a Request for Information (RFI) versus a Request for Proposal (RFP) is typically very different. A RFI is usually issued when an organization is not certain what type of solution is the best fit to meet its requirements; as a result requirements are often presented at a high level and may focus on target outcomes. An RFP is typically used when the organization believes it knows what type of solution it wants and contains very detailed requirements that must be met by a vendor offering a solution.

Once a requirements package is created, it can be communicated to its intended audience.

4.5 Communicate Requirements

Requirements are communicated by Business Analysts throughout the initiative they are working on. Such communication usually happens through a combination of formal and informal methods.

When communicating requirements you also need to convey an understanding of what the current state of the requirements are. Requirements are typically communicated when they are:

■ **Unconfirmed:** the requirements were documented from an elicitation activity but have not yet been confirmed as correct;

■ **Confirmed:** the requirements have been confirmed to have been documented correctly;

- **Verified:** the requirement have been deemed to be of sufficient quality to be used in further activities;
- **Validated:** the requirement has been traced to business requirements that are in scope of the initiative;
- **Prioritized:** the requirements have been prioritized;
- **Approved:** the requirements have been approved.

Requirements may exist in one or more of these states when they are communicated to stakeholders.

> **Example:** Unconfirmed requirements gathered during an elicitation activity are often informally communicated through e-mail or verbal conversations to confirm they have been correctly recorded prior to their use in subsequent tasks (see Section 3.4).

Communicating requirements occurs in most other business analysis tasks. Tasks where requirements communication is particularly integral to successful completion include:

- **Confirm elicitation results (3.4):** elicited requirements may be communicated to ensure they have been accurately recorded;
- **Manage solution scope and requirements (4.1):** requirements are communicated for approval;
- **Define business case (5.5):** requirements are communicated in conjunction with an assessment of why action should be taken to address the requirements;
- **Prioritize requirements (6.1):** requirements are provided to stakeholders to assist in their prioritization;
- **Assess proposed solution (7.1):** requirements are communicated to stakeholders involved in determining which solution to select.

Tip: You may end up using multiple communication methods (for example, a presentation and an associated document) to convey requirements to your audience in order to ensure all individuals have sufficient understanding of the information. If using multiple communication methods, it is important to ensure the requirement details are consistent within each method.

5 Enterprise Analysis

Enterprise analysis answers several fundamental questions that drive an organization to undertake a project or initiative:

- What's the problem (or opportunity)?
- Why do we need to solve the problem?
- How can we go about solving the problem?
- What does our solution need to contain in order to address the problem?

Enterprise analysis activities usually start at the beginning of, or prior to, a new initiative; they provide the context needed to be able to deliver a solution that meets the needs that have been identified.

There are five main tasks involved in Enterprise Analysis:

1. **Define business need:** establish exactly what the problem or opportunity is.
2. **Assess capability gaps:** understand what the organization can do today to meet the business need and identify any additional capabilities necessary in order to fully address the need.
3. **Determine solution approach:** describe how the organization will go about developing a solution to meet the business need. This is different from defining what the solution will be.

4. **Define solution scope:** describe what capabilities the project or initiative needs to deliver in order to address the capability gaps.
5. **Define business case:** assess whether the investment required to deliver the solution is worth it given the anticipated benefits.

The outputs of enterprise analysis are used to guide and shape all other business analysis activities.

5.1   Define Business Need

The business need is the foundation for understanding why a change is needed. Having a clearly defined business need allows you to:

■ Establish whether it is worth pursuing a solution to meet the business need;
■ Plan what additional business analysis activities are required;
■ Understand which stakeholders are involved or impacted and where to elicit requirements from;
■ Prioritize and verify requirements.

Business needs may be initially identified by anyone in the organization. The initial information provided may be vague or incomplete. The Business Analyst can supplement the information provided by assessing the root cause of the problem, reviewing what other organizations are doing (benchmarking) and meeting with relevant stakeholders to gain insight or more detail into the nature of the problem.

The Business Analyst structures the information from stakeholders and other sources to ensure the business need describes:

■ What the issue is in terms of its impact on the organization;
■ The expected outcome of addressing the need and/or the effect of not addressing the need;
■ How the need relates to the organization's goals and objectives.

Where possible, the problem and expected outcome should be described in measurable terms. If an initiative is undertaken to address the business need, the organization can evaluate whether the need is in fact being addressed by the solution implemented.

5.2 Assess Capability Gaps

Once the need has been defined, the Business Analyst needs to understand what capabilities are needed by the organization in order to meet the need.

> **Note:** Capabilities represent the structure, people, processes and technology the organization has to support its business goals and objectives.

In order to determine what gaps exist, if any, a future state of the organization is needed. The future state defines what the organization will look like once the need has been addressed, and includes relevant:

■ Products/services delivered by the organization;
■ Functions/processes that support the delivery of products and services;
■ Roles, organizational structures, and technology executing the functions.

If the organization already has all the capabilities needed to address the business need, then a solution can be implemented by coordinating the required capabilities to solve the problem. However, new capabilities may also be required in order to meet the business need.

Business Analysts can assess current capabilities by:

■ Reviewing existing documentation that defines the organization's capabilities;

■ Engaging with stakeholders to identify and define undocumented
   or under-documented capabilities.

Once the current capabilities are reviewed, the Business Analyst can
identify and describe the missing capabilities the organization needs
in order to meet the change.

> **Tip:** Document your assumptions when assessing whether a capability
> can address a need. There is a risk that an assumption will be incorrect;
> such risks should be addressed through a risk management strategy.

5.3   Determine Solution Approach

A solution approach describes how the organization will go about
developing new capabilities to meet the business need. This is not
the same as defining what the solution will actually be; the approach
describes the general type of solution and its main components.

> **Example:** A solution approach could state a commercial off-the-
> shelf information system will be purchased. The solution itself would
> be the specific system purchased.

Some considerations that may be involved in a particular approach
are:
☑ **People:** will the organizational structure change? Are new roles
   required? Will existing roles be given different responsibilities?
☑ **Process:** are new processes being defined? Are existing processes
   being changed?
☑ **Technology:** is there a need for new technology, or can existing
   technology be used as-is or repurposed? If new technology is to
   be acquired, will it be purchased, developed in-house or some
   combination thereof?

☑ **External Stakeholders:** are there suppliers, vendors or partners required?

☑ **Methodology:** what methodology will be used to implement the required capabilities?

In order to determine what approach to take, several approaches must be evaluated. Examples of the evaluation criteria for determining which approach to take may include:

- The estimated costs and benefits of each approach;
- Qualitative assessments on the value of each approach;
- Constraints on possible solutions or on allowed approaches within the organization;
- The general feasibility of possible solutions entailed by a given approach.

Once a solution approach has been selected, the solution's scope can be defined.

5.4   Define Solution Scope

The solution scope describes what exactly will be delivered in a solution. The solution scope must demonstrate how the solution:

- Meets the business need;
- Contains the required capabilities;
- Adheres to the solution approach defined.

> **Note:** The solution scope is kept high level and maps major solution components to business requirements. Stakeholder and solution requirements are mapped to specific solution features in Section 7.2.

Part of the solution scope is the implementation approach, which describes what parts of the solution will be provided when. This is useful when the solution is either implemented in stages or delivered to different stakeholders at different times.

> **Tip:** The solution scope is about more than simply describing the main technology features being developed. Organizational structures, roles and business processes must also be included, as well as any relevant dependencies between the components.

5.5   Define Business Case

The business case describes the value a proposed project is expected to bring to the organization. Business cases are often used to determine whether the organization should proceed with larger project. When an organization has multiple opportunities to pursue but only limited resources, business cases are often compared between one another to determine which initiatives will move forward.

A business case will contain at least the following elements:

- **Benefits:** the anticipated quantitative and qualitative benefits the solution will deliver;
- **Costs:** the financial cost of creating and implementing the solution, and any potential qualitative costs as well;
- **Opportunities and Risk Assessment:** an evaluation of the potential positive and negative variations from the expected outcomes. All qualitative and quantitative cost and benefit areas should be considered and, where possible, include a probability of variation.

Tip: When performing qualitative analysis, potential qualitative costs are often overlooked but should also be included. For example, an oil company may consider the qualitative cost to their reputation or brand if they are planning a new project in an environmentally sensitive area.

Many organizations will have quantitative assessment criteria for projects of a certain size to determine whether a project should proceed or not. In addition to the relative value of the project, it may need to meet a certain threshold for its return on investment in order to be considered.

Tip: Ensure that the business case includes measures to evaluate the success of the project.

6 Requirements Analysis

Requirements analysis takes a set of requirements and analyzes them in order to understand what an organization needs to solve a problem, identify possible opportunities for improvement, or to better understand how the organization works. There are six Requirements Analysis tasks:

1. **Prioritize requirements:** take a collection of requirements and define a relative or absolute priority amongst them.

2. **Organize requirements:** define how requirements will be modeled and how multiple models are inter-related. This serves as the blueprint for how to present requirements to stakeholders.

3. **Specify and model requirements:** describe the requirements using a combination of text, models and other structures to convey pertinent details about the requirements.

4. **Define assumptions and constraints:** identify and record factors that can affect the possible solutions to the problem.

5. **Verify requirements:** ensure requirement specifications and models meet quality criteria so they can be used within other business analysis activities.

6. **Validate requirements:** tie requirements that are within the scope of the solution back to business requirements to ensure they are relevant to the objectives of the initiative.

6.1   Prioritize Requirements

An initiative rarely has the time, money, or resources to address all possible requirements that fall within its scope. Requirements are prioritized to make the best use of scarce resources and to evaluate potential solutions. When prioritizing requirements, the Business Analyst has to consider the following:

☑ What ranking or scale will be used for prioritizing requirements? A relative scale such as 'High/Medium/Low', something more absolute like 'Mandatory/Optional', an ordered list from the top priority to the lowest priority, or some combination can be used.

☑ Who needs to be involved in the prioritization process? Certain individuals or groups may have to be included given their role in the initiative, while others may be consulted for their opinion but will not be included in the decision process.

☑ What are the aspects that will be used as the basis for prioritization? Items such as level of effort, cost, risk, difficulty, regulatory compliance, and value may be used as a basis for determining the priority of each requirement.

☑ How will rankings be determined? Rankings could be determined by a formula based on inputs from the prioritization aspects and stakeholder assessments. Alternatively, a voting or consultation/decision process could be used.

> ⚠ **Example:** When a budget or schedule is fixed the team can start with all requirements that are in or out of scope for implementation and then, one by one, add or remove requirements until the budget or schedule is met. The team may then evaluate whether it is worth proceeding based on what can actually be accomplished.

Tip: Once a prioritization activity has taken place using a relative ranking system, it is important to review the results to ensure they are usable. When nearly all requirements are given the same relative ranking (for example 'High') further prioritization is likely to be needed if the solution can't accommodate all the requirements with the same ranking.

6.2 Organize Requirements

Requirements are organized so they can be presented to stakeholders for their use. Different stakeholders may need a different representation or view of the requirements. For example:

- Individuals who need to develop a solution need requirements organized in a way that describes what they need to build;
- Sponsors and leaders need to understand at a high level what requirements are being addressed by the solution and that the detailed requirements sufficiently cover the objectives of the initiative;
- End users need requirements organized so they can understand what solution they will receive;
- Teams of Business Analysts need requirements organized so they can assess possible solutions, identify opportunities, and easily maintain requirements during the initiative;
- Auditors or other regulatory bodies want to see how an organization has implemented a solution to address certain requirements.

Note: Requirements may be presented at various levels of abstraction depending on the audience. For example, detailed stakeholder and solution requirements may be abstracted to an aggregate function or feature level when reviewing a possible solution offering with executives.

A requirements structure describes how requirements are organized so that information can be found and/or viewed by any relevant stakeholder involved in the initiative. The structure is the framework for specifying and modeling requirements. The structure should address the following:

☑ Is each type of different model or artifact within the structure defined?

☑ If there is a need for reference documentation that describes how certain models or requirements are laid out in the structure, is it included?

☑ Do stakeholders know which models or other artifacts within the structure are relevant to them?

☑ Are the relationships between various models and artifacts within the structure clearly described?

☑ If the same requirements are presented in multiple ways within the structure, are their representations consistent?

Tip: Different types of models may be used to represent the same information to different audiences. Select a model that provides sufficient detail for the requirements but is also already understood by the audience, or can be easily taught to them.

6.3   Specify and Model Requirements

This task takes requirements and puts them in a specific representation for a particular purpose, for example:

■ To analyze the current state of an organization;

■ To present requirements to stakeholders for feedback;

■ To assess what potential solutions can address the requirements;

■ To map requirements to tests that are used in order to ensure the solution actually meets the requirements.

There are several ways to represent requirements:

- **Text:** a description of a requirement in a language common to all stakeholders. Text is often used to specify requirements, however there are risks that requirements can be misinterpreted by different audiences reading the same text.
- **Matrices:** a structured array which can be used to show relationships between requirements, or to list a set of requirements. For example, a matrix may be used to list all requirements along with attributes such as who originally indicated the requirement, its priority, current status, and so on.
- **Models:** a simplification of reality that provides insight into how the organization or system operates. There are many types of models that can be used, ranging from screenshots, mock-ups and prototypes to notations, symbols and diagrams. Models can be an excellent way to convey detailed and complex information in a condensed representation. However, there is a possibility for confusion or misinterpretation if the audience is not familiar with the model's conventions or notation.

Note: Business Analysts often use formally defined models and notations to represent requirements. Some of the typical standards in use today include Unified Modeling Language (UML), Business Process Modeling Notation (BPMN), Data Flow Diagrams, the Zachman Framework and The Open Group Architectural Framework (TOGAF).

As with other tasks such as Organize Requirements (Section 6.2) and Prepare Requirements Package (Section 4.4), the specific representation to be used in a particular situation depends on several key factors:

- ☑ Who is the recipient of the specified and modeled requirements?
- ☑ What will the recipient do with the specified and modeled requirements?

- ☑ What information needs to be represented?
- ☑ Based on the audience and how they intend to use the requirements, what is the scope and complexity of the information that needs to be represented?
- ☑ Does the audience sufficiently understand the terminology and conventions used in the requirements representation so there is a minimal chance of misinterpretations, confusion or other issues with their consumption of the requirements?
- ☑ If not all information within the scope of the solution is included in the representation, how will the audience know what has been excluded or that the included requirements are complete for their purposes?

Tip: Whenever you need to specify and model requirements, ensure the 'Keep it Simple' principle is at the front of your mind. If there is a choice between a complex modeling notation and a simpler option, choose the simpler version. If some information can be left out of the requirements collection because it is not relevant, then do so. Audiences are often overloaded with complex and very detailed requirements representations that do not achieve their intended objective because it is impossible to process the vast amount of information provided.

6.4   Define Assumptions and Constraints

While requirements are a key component of assessing problems and determining possible solutions, there are two other factors that often affect business analysis activities:

- **Assumptions:** concepts that are currently considered to be true, but have not been verified. An assumption is considered a risk if there is a potential to negatively affect the initiative should the assumption turn out to be false.

- **Constraints:** a restriction or limitation that affects possible solutions. Constraints may set boundaries for what types of solutions might be considered, represent limits on the amount available to spend on a solution, or place controls on how the solution can be used.

Assumptions and constraints are usually identified when eliciting requirements from stakeholders. There are two types of constraints: business and technical constraints.

Business constraints are not solution-specific; they represent internal or external limits that affect the potential solutions delivered. Business constraints can be:
- Budget or time limits;
- Resources that can be used in the initiative;
- Laws or regulations that prohibit certain types of solutions to be considered;
- Imposed scope boundaries.

Technical constraints describe limits that affect the type of solution or certain components of the solution. These can include:
- Solution procurement approach (buying an off-the-shelf solution versus developing in-house);
- Mandated technologies to use (hardware, software, infrastructure);
- Inability to reorganize the corporate structure to improve processes;
- Network or infrastructure limits (bandwidth);
- Existing contracted service level agreements.

> **Tip:** Even though assumptions and constraints are not requirements, they also need to be managed through the lifecycle of the initiative. Assumptions should be evaluated and attempts made to verify them, while constraints should be monitored in case they are no longer valid.

Since assumptions and constraints affect the development of a solution, they need to be included with requirements in certain requirements packages and communications so that solution implementers are aware of their existence.

6.5 Verify Requirements

Requirements are verified to ensure their quality is sufficient to be used in other tasks. Poor quality requirements are more likely to result in misinterpretations, confusion and rework. Requirements should be verified by Business Analysts before they are communicated to stakeholders, although other stakeholders may also verify the requirements.

There are key criteria that can be used to ensure requirements are of a high quality:

- ☑ **Cohesive:** all requirements in a collection are relevant to the scope and purpose of the initiative;
- ☑ **Complete:** each requirement is self-sufficient on its own, and all requirements in a collection are all that are needed to perform the desired activity;
- ☑ **Consistent:** requirements do not contradict one another;
- ☑ **Correct:** the detail of each requirement is truthful;
- ☑ **Feasible:** each requirement represents a need that can reasonably be met given the scope and constraints of the solution;
- ☑ **Modifiable:** requirements are structured so they can be changed while maintaining consistency and correctness;

☑ **Unambiguous:** each requirement is understandable and cannot be interpreted in more than one way;

☑ **Testable:** there is a way to ensure the requirement has been met by the solution.

Tip: There may be different ways of applying these criteria depending on the audience for the requirements and their intended use of requirements. For example, using a formal modeling notation to represent requirements may ensure they are unambiguous to a solution team but may make the requirements unintelligible to executives.

You can verify requirements with several different techniques:

■ Completeness can be checked by reviewing conditions and options within the requirements to ensure every scenario is accounted for;

■ Requirements that have been represented in multiple ways (for example, with text, graphics and/or a picture) should be reviewed to ensure each representation is consistent with one another;

■ Feasibility can be verified in discussions with the solution team;

■ Test criteria can be written for each requirement to ensure it is clear and evident when the requirement has been met;

■ Text-based requirements can be reviewed by multiple individuals to ensure they all interpret the information in the same way;

■ Each requirement's attributes are checked to ensure all required information is recorded;

■ Where structured models have been used, ensure that all necessary features are implemented.

Example: A convention used in various process modeling standards is that each process should have its inputs, outputs, preconditions and post conditions listed with the process to ensure completeness.

6.6　Validate Requirements

Requirements are validated to ensure they are relevant to the scope of the initiative and are justified by tying back to the business requirements that represent the goals and objectives of the organization.

Business Analysts often elicit more requirements than are relevant to the initiative they are working on. Some of the requirements may be easily set aside if they are clearly out of scope, but others may appear to be in scope. Validating requirements ensures that when requirements are addressed by the solution they actually deliver value to the organization. Value can be represented in many forms:

■ A financial return on investment, which considers the cost of implementing a solution for the requirement and the future savings or increased revenue as a result of meeting the requirement;
■ Conformance with mandatory external standards and regulations, or internal policies and standards;
■ Increased satisfaction by customers;
■ Greater brand value or awareness;
■ Improved consistency in service or product delivery.

> **Example:** A project is implementing a new Enterprise Resource Planning system. A stakeholder has requested that existing reports be recreated in the new system. However, upon reviewing the reports, several are identified as no longer being used by any process or in any decision making activities.

The business case for an initiative can be used to help evaluate whether requirements are valid. If a business case was not created, you can use other available documents such as:

■ Vision and mission statements;
■ Business plan;

- Operating plans;
- Key performance indicators.

> **Tip:** Some requirements when viewed in isolation may not appear to deliver business value. Ensure you trace relationships between requirements so that those requirements which have indirect value are not incorrectly removed from the scope of your analysis.

Requirements should be validated before solutions are assessed; otherwise certain solutions may appear more or less attractive based on requirements that are not relevant.

7 Solution Assessment and Validation

Solution assessment and validation involves determining how well potential solutions meet the organization's requirements, facilitating the implementation of a chosen solution, and evaluating how well a solution is performing once it is in place.

> **Note:** A Business Analyst may perform solution assessment and validation techniques not only on software systems but also on business processes, service agreements, organizational and governance structures, and other solution components.

There are six Solution Assessment and Validation tasks:

1. **Assess proposed solution:** review a solution's features and evaluate how well they are able to meet the requirements in scope of the initiative;

2. **Allocate requirements:** map the requirements to specific components of a solution and to specific releases of the solution, if the solution is not being implemented all at once;

3. **Assess organizational readiness:** determine how prepared the organization is to implement the changes that will occur as part of the introduction of the new solution;

4. **Define transition requirements:** define requirements that are needed to implement the new solution from the current state, but that are not needed once the new solution is in place;
5. **Validate solution:** ensure that a constructed solution meets its stated specifications and requirements;
6. **Evaluate solution performance:** determine how well an implemented solution is operating and look for potential improvements.

7.1   Assess Proposed Solution

Once requirements have been approved and prioritized, potential solutions can be assessed. Upon completion of the assessment, you may recommend a solution to be implemented, or you may find that no solution delivers sufficient value to warrant its investment.

Solution assessment usually involves the following steps:
- The solution's capabilities are evaluated to see if they address the specified requirements;
- Where the solution does not meet the requirements, the gap is assessed to determine its impact and identify possible workarounds or alternatives;
- Criteria unrelated to requirements are evaluated, for example the solution's financial cost, the reputation and viability of the solution provider, and the possibility of solution components becoming obsolete or breaking down over time;
- The evaluation criteria are combined to determine the relative value of the potential solution.

There may be some mandatory criteria that must be met. These criteria are often evaluated first to arrive at a go/no-go decision before taking more time to fully assess possible solutions.

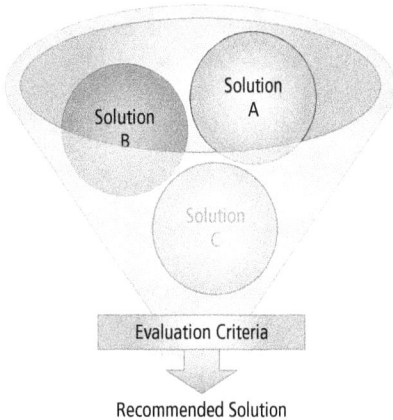

Figure 7.1 Evaluation of potential solutions

Each evaluation criterion is usually assigned a score and a weighting. The scoring may be based on quantitative or qualitative measures, for example:

- The anticipated financial cost or return on investment;
- The percentage of non-mandatory requirements met;
- The degree to which reference customers who have purchased the solution indicated they are happy with their decision;
- The feedback received from internal reviewers who trialed the solution;
- The number of defects reported by other customers per year;
- The perceived quality of the solution components;

The weighted scores provide a relative anticipated value for each possible solution. Depending on the scoring and weighting methods used, the organization may wish to perform supplementary evaluations if two or more possible solutions have very similar results.

> **Tip:** Constraints may become evaluation criteria as they can restrict possible solution options. Assumptions may influence how certain solutions are valued – if the assumptions have not been validated before evaluation their impact on the assessment should be noted as part of the recommendation summary.

7.2 Allocate Requirements

Allocating requirements takes requirements and traces them to the capabilities of the solution that will be used to address them. Some requirements may be addressed by a collection of solution capabilities.

Requirements allocation can be done to facilitate solution assessment (see Section 7.1) or to help an implementation team design and build a solution. If a solution is being built, requirements allocation is done iteratively as the solution design is refined and implementation begins.

> **Note:** In the context of building a solution that will be deployed incrementally, requirements can be allocated between different releases. In this scenario the allocation activity is meant to determine what requirements will be addressed when.

When allocating requirements, all solution components are mapped to clearly identify how each requirement will be met. This includes:

- Business processes;
- Organizational roles and units;
- External organizations;
- Business policies and rules;
- Information systems.

> **Tip:** The solution does not have to be built to have requirements
> allocated, but it needs to have been designed at some level so there is an
> understanding of which components are expected to address each
> requirement.

Once requirements have been allocated, the resulting solution
roadmap can be evaluated:

☑ Are there requirements not addressed by the solution? If so, how
   is the organization affected if these requirements remain unmet?
   Can existing solution components be adapted to meet any of these
   requirements?

☑ Is the solution implementation plan cost-effective? Some
   components could be expensive to acquire while addressing only
   low priority requirements.

☑ Does the implementation order make sense? There may be
   dependencies that have not yet been captured in the solution
   design which result in some components being delivered before
   they can be used because they rely on other components in order to
   be relevant.

☑ Are there resourcing challenges? Some resources may be
   overloaded during the implementation of the solution that will
   impact planned timelines, or certain business units may have
   excess capacity once the entire solution is operational.

7.3   Assess Organizational Readiness

Implementing a new solution in an organization involves change.
Before the solution can be successfully implemented, the individuals
within the organization who are affected by the change need to be
collectively on board with the change, or it is much more likely to
fail. Similarly, the organization needs to be technically capable of
completing the implementation of the solution and supporting its
operation after it is in place.

Business Analysts can help facilitate a successful change by assessing the organization's readiness to change and subsequently defining transitional requirements that describe what the organization needs in order to implement the change. See figure 7.2.

Figure 7.2 Organizational readiness factors

There are four main components to consider as part of the organizational readiness assessment:
- ☑ What is the nature of the change? What is the scale and scope of the change; how broad is its effect on the overall organization?
- ☑ Who and what are affected by the change? Which people, organizational units, processes and technology?
- ☑ What is the organization's ability to implement the change, both in terms of the people, its current process, and technological maturity?
- ☑ What is the organization's willingness to implement the change? What are the main factors that play into their willingness and how could those factors change over the course of the initiative?

Tip: An early readiness assessment can be used during the development of the business case to evaluate how likely the organization will be able to successfully implement a new solution, and also during solution evaluation to identify potential solutions that may have a higher risk of implementation failure.

Once the people and organizational units that will be affected by the change are identified, each individual, unit, or the organization as a whole can be evaluated over the following characteristics to determine their ability and willingness for change:

- Belief in the need for a solution to the problem or opportunity;
- Visible leadership support for the solution implementation;
- Ability of staff who will need to use the solution to adapt to the proposed changes;
- Amount of change already occurring within the organization and how well the organization is adapting;
- Previous failures that may impact upon opinions about the proposed implementation.

Tip: If you work in an organization that regularly starts initiatives for new solutions, it is worthwhile developing scoring criteria for organizational readiness characteristics. This will help you and management to understand the scale and scope of each proposed change and also enable better management of upcoming changes from an overall portfolio perspective.

Technical readiness can also be assessed to ensure the organization has the skills and capacity to adopt technology as part of the new solution. Factors that play into technical readiness include:

- The nature of existing systems that are being replaced or retired as part of the change;

- The amount of data that needs to be moved from current information systems to new information systems;
- Whether the organization has in-house expertise in the new technology or whether it will need to acquire expertise through hiring, retraining or outsourcing.

7.4   Define Transition Requirements

Transition requirements are capabilities needed by the organization to move from its current state to a future state that contains the new solution, but are no longer required once the new solution is in place. Transition requirements define what is needed in order to successfully complete the adoption of the new solution.

Developing transition requirements leverages the organizational readiness assessment and the current and future solutions. Some typical considerations for transition requirements are:

☑ What sort of training is required to ensure staff are able to use the new solution?

☑ How will data be migrated from the current to the new solution?

☑ What will happen to the old solution once the new solution is up and running?

☑ If both solutions are to be in simultaneous operation for a period of time, how will the organization function during this period?

☑ How will staff, suppliers and customers be kept up to date on the progress of the transition based on their level of involvement and what the changes mean to them, and where can they get help or more information?

☑ How and when will changes to the organizational structure occur?

Note: Transition requirements are managed like any other type of requirement. Once elicited, they must be verified, validated, reviewed and approved.

7.5   Validate Solution

Once a solution has been built (but is not necessarily in use), it can
be tested to ensure it meets the defined requirements. Validating a
solution involves determining how the solution will be evaluated,
performing evaluation testing, documenting and analyzing the results,
and determining how to resolve any problems that are identified. See
figure 7.3.

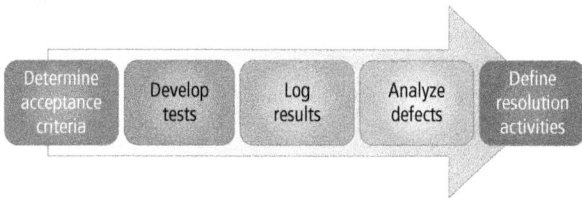

Figure 7.3 Solution validation activities

> **Tip:** Depending on the scale of the solution it may be impossible to
> validate the solution against all requirements. Requirements need to be
> prioritized prior to solution validation to ensure that, at a minimum, the
> critical requirements are validated.

After testing is performed, there are two main types of defects that
may arise:

■ The solution may not behave as expected when used for a given
  purpose or provided with a given input;
■ The solution performs its functions correctly, but the quality of its
  processes or outputs is deemed to be insufficient.

> ⚠️ **Example:** To process an insurance claim an adjuster needs to navigate between three screens instead of having all the information on one screen. The system provides all required information and can properly enter and store the data, but the organization is dissatisfied with the layout of the information.

Once problems are identified, the Business Analyst needs to determine how they will be addressed. Typically there are two possible ways to address these problems:

■ Modify the solution to resolve the problem;
■ Develop a method to mitigate the problem.

> 📝 **Note:** Mitigation options can include creating additional quality checks to verify correctness, developing workaround steps, or deciding the solution will not perform certain activities until the defects are resolved.

Once all testing is performed and the defects are identified, an overall solution assessment can be performed. The assessment should highlight whether the solution fully meets the business need, the severity and effect of any identified defects and, if the solution is not yet implemented, whether to proceed with deployment.

7.6   Evaluate Solution Performance

Once a solution is in place it can be evaluated to determine how well it is working. In order to assess the solution performance measures need to be defined. Performance measures may be a combination of quantitative and qualitative results. Some examples include:

■ Number of correct outputs generated over some time period;
■ Processing time to perform a certain function;
■ Satisfaction survey from individuals who interact with the solution, or from customers who use the product of the solution;

- Known defects and their effects on the organization's operations;
- Amount of revenue generated or costs avoided.

> **Tip:** The performance measures chosen for the evaluation need to be relevant to the business requirements that the solution is supposed to address. Map the selected measures to the relevant business requirements and validate this mapping with stakeholders prior to gathering the data for the performance metrics.

Similar to assessing proposed solutions (see Section 7.1), performance measures can be scored and weighted to aggregate the results and determine the absolute or relative value of the solution to the organization. If a solution does not meet a certain threshold or scores low compared to other solutions in use by the organization, it may be a candidate for replacement or elimination. Some considerations that factor into the decision include:

- How essential is the solution to the organization's objectives?
- What alternatives are there available to replace the solution? What are their costs and benefits?
- If a replacement is pursued, what is the opportunity cost (what else could the organization do with the resources spent on replacing the solution)?
- How much longer is the solution anticipated to be needed? At some point could the need for any solution no longer be necessary?

> **Note:** If replacement is viewed as a possibility based on the solution's performance assessment, enterprise analysis (see Chapter 5) can be performed to determine whether there is a justifiable business case for pursuing an alternative solution.

8 Underlying Competencies

Performing business analysis tasks effectively requires having certain fundamental abilities, characteristics and skills. Being a Business Analyst means you need to be able to work in different organizational environments and cultures, understand how to work with and influence a variety of people, and mix analytical thinking with creativity to deliver value to stakeholders. As a result Business Analysts draw from a wide range of competencies. See figure 8.1.

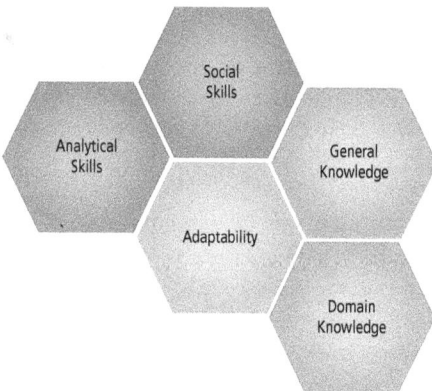

Figure 8.1 Business analysis competencies

In general there are five types of competencies used when performing business analysis:

1. **Analytical Skills:** you can't be an analyst without analytical skills. Analysis involves being able to take materials and break them down into their constituent parts in order to understand each part and the inter-relationships with one another.

2. **Social Skills:** performing business analysis involves engaging with a wide variety of people. Social skills are needed to effectively interact with others and gain insights into the organization's problems and opportunities.

3. **Adaptability:** business analysis activities are moulded to the context of the particular problem or opportunity being analyzed, the organizational environment and the culture of the stakeholders. As a result Business Analysts need to be able to adapt their methods and approaches, and also adapt to the evolving and optimizing practice of business analysis itself.

4. **General Knowledge:** business analysis requires a fundamental understanding of how organizations work, market economics, and information technologies and their capabilities.

5. **Domain Knowledge:** business analysis is always undertaken in the context of a particular organization, which requires an understanding of the organization, its industry, and the regulatory or political environments that govern how the organization can address its needs.

8.1   *BABOK® Guide* Underlying Competencies

The *BABOK® Guide* has six categories of underlying competencies:

1. **Analytical Thinking and Problem Solving**
   - **Creative thinking:** find new and innovative ways to solve problems or address issues;
   - **Decision making**: consider all relevant information and options to arrive at a reasonable and thoughtful decision;

- **Learning:** gain new knowledge and skills to better understand the organization, perform business analysis activities, or engage stakeholders;
- **Problem solving:** ensure root cause(s) are understood and come up with a solution to address the problem;
- **Systems thinking:** understand how people, processes and technology work together and the effects of changes to one or more components of a larger whole.

2. **Behavioral Characteristics**
   - **Ethics:** have a set of principles for appropriate conduct and apply them to working on an initiative;
   - **Personal organization:** manage information and tasks in a methodical manner that allows tasks to be performed in a consistent and timely way;
   - **Trustworthiness:** be viewed as a reliable individual by stakeholders who believe you will be able to perform your duties in an appropriate fashion.

3. **Business Knowledge**
   - **Business principles and practices:** have an understanding of how most organizations generally operate;
   - **Industry knowledge:** able to comprehend the common characteristics and trends facing all organizations that provide similar goods or services;
   - **Organization knowledge:** understand the behaviors and characteristics of a particular organization, ranging from its goals and purpose to its business models, operations and the relationships within and outside of the organization;
   - **Solution knowledge:** understand the solutions that are currently in place within an organization in order to be able to find ways to improve upon them.

4. **Communications Skills**
   - **Oral communications:** able to deliver information clearly through verbal methods;
   - **Teaching:** help others to understand concepts, absorb information and develop their skills to support their learning;
   - **Written communications:** convey information clearly through documentation, messages and other written methods.

5. **Interaction Skills**
   - **Facilitation:** make it easier for stakeholders to work together to accomplish a task;
   - **Negotiation:** work with or on behalf of others to arrive at a decision or agreement between competing interests;
   - **Leadership:** have others willing to take direction and/or follow you, regardless of your defined role in the formal organizational structure;
   - **Influencing:** affect the decisions and opinions of others;
   - **Teamwork:** perform activities in combination with others in a cohesive manner.

6. **Software Skills**
   - **General purpose applications:** able to use standard operating systems on modern devices as well as basic office productivity software, communication tools and collaboration applications;
   - **Specialized applications:** software that can be used to support business analysis activities.

8.2   Additional Competencies

In addition to the *BABOK® Guide* competencies, the following competencies are also of value to Business Analysts.

Strategic Thinking

Strategic thinking is a method to find innovative and effective ways to meet the objectives of the organization. The purpose of strategic thinking is to develop an integrated view of the enterprise that increases the ability of the thinker to find opportunities to enhance the organization[3].

There are five elements within strategic thinking that help drive one's ability to think in this manner[4]:

1. **A systems perspective:** in order to think strategically, systems thinking is required to understand how the inter-relationships and nature of various components affect an overall operation.
2. **Intent focused:** strategic thinking services a purpose and is targeted at achieving a certain goal.
3. **Intelligent opportunism:** strategic thinking relies on the ability to shift from the current beliefs and strategies in place to better and more effective options if they present themselves, within the context of the overall intent.
4. **Thinking in time:** bringing together relevant lessons from the past, the current status of the organization and the future intent in order to determine the best path forward.
5. **Hypothesis-driven:** developing a possible explanation for how to operate and then deriving methods to test this hypothesis allows a mixture of analytical and creative thinking to drive actions.

> **Note:** Business Analysts who use strategic thinking are able to see the potential value in possible solutions and opportunities as they relate to the organization's overall objectives. These opportunities may lie outside of the current initiative, but should be appropriately communicated to others in the organization so they can be assessed and acted upon accordingly.

Financial Knowledge

Business Analysts who can provide quantitative-driven analysis when performing enterprise analysis, solution assessment and performance evaluations deliver enhanced value to their organizations, particularly in relation to entities that rely on corporate finance methodologies to drive internal and external investment decisions.

Key financial knowledge competencies include:

- **Time value of money:** understanding how currencies depreciate in value over time is important when analyzing initiatives where the investment costs and potential returns last over several years;
- **Basic return calculations:** being able to calculate the quantitative returns expected for an initiative through methods such as net present value and the internal rate of return help to frame a business case in a context familiar to senior executives;
- **Economic theory:** models to represent potential supply and demand, price elasticity, and understanding the economic value of sunk costs can help shape quantitative benefit predictions;
- **Probability theory:** enables a more rigorous analysis of potential outcomes and risks through the use of non-deterministic models and simulation techniques;
- **Portfolio management:** helps to understand the relative value of potential initiatives and options given their risk/reward profiles.

8.3   Additional Behavioral Characteristics
Cool Under Pressure

Business Analysts can be faced with stress-filled situations on a daily basis. Whether it is difficult stakeholders, tight deadlines, or needing to act with only incomplete information available, you can be under constant pressure to constantly deliver high quality results.

Being able to handle high stress situations without outwardly exhibiting the effects of the stress to stakeholders and team members is a key leadership trait that will allow others to believe in your work and abilities. While the outcome of your efforts may not always be successful, it is important to believe in your ability to deliver the best possible result given the circumstances and share that belief with those you are working with.

Inquisitive

In order to properly perform the learning competency (competence) described in the *BABOK® Guide*, a Business Analyst must be innately inquisitive. Wanting to learn about the underlying causes of things, events and actions as well as being open to new knowledge will allow you to develop broad horizons and a multi-disciplined approach to performing business analysis.

Inquisitiveness allows you to continually improve yourself, your organization and those you work with, while increasing your ability to obtain new business and software skills as the world evolves over time.

Personally Engaging

An engaging personality is a behavioral characteristic where the person is considered pleasant, interesting and entertaining[5]. If you are engaging, other people *want* to interact with you; they consciously or unconsciously are more willing to make time to work with you, respond to your questions to help you out.

Engaging Business Analysts leverage their communication and interaction skills to accomplish their activities more efficiently. While some individuals may have an inherently more engaging personality than others, there are some underlying behaviors that can drive how engaging you are perceived, many of which overlap with other business analysis competencies:

■ Have a broad set of knowledge from various disciplines and fields;

- Leverage creative thinking to put forward a unique perspective;
- Demonstrate empathy towards others;
- Are passionate and enthusiastic about their work;
- Can find humor in most situations.

8.4   Complementary Disciplines

Having expertise in other disciplines can be used to enhance your ability to perform business analysis. While you may never have worked as a dedicated specialist in any of the roles below, the following disciplines represent related fields that provide valuable skills and techniques for Business Analysts in their daily activities.

Project Management

A project is the temporary group of activities designed to produce a unique product, service or result[6]. Project Management is the application of knowledge to execute projects effectively and efficiently. The Project Management Institute's *PMBOK Guide* contains several techniques and knowledge areas relevant to business analysis:

- **Planning:** central to project management is the creation, monitoring and control of a project through a project plan. Business analysts can learn how to enhance business analysis plans by understanding how to create and use plans that involve multiple inter-related and dependent activities, estimate effort and the time activities will take, and assess the impact of changes to the plan.
- **Financial management:** Project Managers need to be able to estimate, control and analyze project costs. Several of the techniques required by Project Managers are valuable to Business Analysts in performing enterprise analysis and solution assessment.
- **People management:** the *PMBOK Guide* includes two knowledge areas, human resources and communications, which provide a great amount of detail on how to support, interact with, and

manage people within the context of an initiative. Business Analysts can enhance their communication and interaction skills through these knowledge areas.

Change Management

Change management (or 'organizational change management', so as not to be confused with the use of the term 'change management' within the information technology domain), deals with the people side of change. Nearly every initiative a Business Analyst embarks upon is likely to result in change for at least one individual within the organization. Change management practices help individuals successfully process change.

Business Analysts can leverage change management techniques to:
- Perform stakeholder analysis that will help in understanding the people who represent barriers to change and the drivers for change within the organization;
- Resolve issues and concerns of stakeholders;
- Elicit transition requirements and develop transition plans that account for the need to address the change process for people;
- Obtain approval for requirements.

Conflict Resolution

Business Analysts who work with multiple stakeholders typically have to deal with some level of conflict during the course of an initiative. Being able to affectively deal with conflicts will reduce the time it takes to successfully complete business analysis tasks.

Conflict resolution techniques have been developed and refined by mediators and arbitrators to arrive at a settlement or understanding that will enable all parties to move forward. Some key competencies held by conflict resolution professionals include:

- The ability to represent themselves as a fair and impartial party to the dispute;
- Ability to facilitate discussion and avoid potential issues arising from emotion-driven positions;
- Identify the root causes of the dispute and the options that will benefit both parties;
- Shift the focus from areas of disagreement to shared views that can be built upon for a complete resolution.

9 Techniques

Techniques describe a way to systematically perform a task. Business Analysts use techniques to achieve repeatable, consistent and appropriate outcomes when performing business analysis activities.

9.1 *BABOK® Guide* General Techniques

The *BABOK® Guide* contains a listing of 34 general techniques that can be used within various business analysis tasks. Throughout the *BABOK® Guide* there are additional techniques described for a specific business analysis task.

The general techniques presented in Chapter 9 of the *BABOK® Guide* can be classified into the categories shown in figure 9.1.

These techniques rely on engaging stakeholders to obtain information that will be used to further the initiative. Most of these techniques are used to perform elicitation, although they can be applied to other activities as well. The techniques are:

- **Brainstorming:** produce as many solution ideas as possible to address a problem;
- **Focus groups:** discuss a specific topic with pre-selected participants;

Figure 9.1 Stakeholder engagement

- **Interviews:** elicit information from one or more people through a series of questions or in an open discussion;
- **Lessons learned process:** hold a session with stakeholders to get feedback on a completed deliverable, task or initiative;
- **Observation:** watch individuals perform their work to understand how an organization currently operates;
- **Requirements workshops:** a structured session where requirements can be elicited, verified, prioritized or reviewed for approval;
- **Structured walkthrough:** review and discuss a specific set of requirements that have been documented and organized;
- **Survey/questionnaire:** a set of written questions or statements sent to stakeholders in order to elicit information.

Modeling Methods
As discussed in Chapter 6.3, a model is a simplification of reality that is used to help people understand how a system or organization

operates. Business Analysts use several modeling methods to convey information about a wide variety of topics, from solution implementation details to high-level descriptions of the organization and its interaction with other entities. The methods include:

- **Data flow diagrams:** show how information moves between and is used by components of a solution;
- **Data modeling:** depict concepts that represent information which is involved in the operation of the organization and its inter-relationships;
- **Functional decomposition:** break down the high-level functions that an organization performs into more detailed descriptions;
- **Organization modeling:** describe how the organization has structured its people, and the roles and responsibilities individuals have;
- **Process modeling:** a visual representation of how an organization performs tasks in a repeatable, consistent manner to perform a specific duty;
- **Prototyping:** a representation of what the solution should look like and how it should behave – the prototype may be able to deliver some level of functionality;
- **Scenarios and use cases:** describe how a stakeholder interacts with a solution to accomplish a goal;
- **Scope modeling:** used to show what is considered in scope for an initiative through the use of visual diagramming;
- **Sequence diagrams:** a graphical view of how components of a (typically software) solution interact to address a specific scenario;
- **State diagrams:** a depiction of the different states an entity can have over its lifetime, and the reasons why it enters and leaves those states;
- **User stories:** concise textual descriptions of what a solution is supposed to do for someone in order to achieve a specific goal.

Assessments

Business Analysts need to be able to come up with recommendations or decisions that take into account the available information about a situation. This can involve using a combination of quantitative and qualitative criteria to come up with a complete assessment based on relevant facts and possible outcomes. The following methods help Business Analysts determine how to reach appropriate conclusions:

- **Acceptance and evaluation criteria definition:** determine under what circumstances a solution will be deemed sufficiently acceptable and/or how to determine which possible solution should be chosen if multiple options exist;
- **Benchmarking:** compare an organization to its competitors to identify what practices are driving superior performance;
- **Decision analysis:** a methodical approach to determine which course of action to take, based on the quantitative assessment of each possible outcome involving financial criteria and probabilities of each outcome;
- **Estimation:** determine the possible cost and effort required to perform an activity – can include developing a range of possible values and their associated probabilities;
- **Strengths, Weaknesses, Opportunities, Threats (SWOT) analysis:** assess the current state of an organization or organizational process and determine what actions could be taken to improve the situation going forward;
- **Vendor assessment:** determine whether a potential vendor will be able to deliver its proposed solution and the implications on the organization if it selects the vendor's solution.

Issue and Risk Management

When embarking on an initiative, there is always the potential that it will not be successful. Risks and issues relate to items that could cause the initiative to fail or affect its degree of success. Risks represent potential negative effects, while issues represent actualized problems that need resolution. Business Analysts need to be able to understand each risk and issue and work with other stakeholders to either mitigate their effect on the initiative or bring about their resolution. This can be achieved through:

- **Problem tracking:** maintain an up-to-date listing of issues and risks so they can be assessed and addressed as required;
- **Risk analysis:** assess risks in the context of the organization and the initiative, and determine what actions to take in order to address the risk;
- **Root cause analysis:** understand the core reasons for an issue in order to be able take appropriate measures that will ensure the issue does not arise in another form.

Organization, Solution and System Analysis

Business Analysts study how people, organizations, processes and technologies work together in order to further the organization's goals. The following analysis techniques further an understanding of an organization and its components:

- **Business rules analysis:** define how an organization is governed by the rules that implement its policies;
- **Data dictionary and glossary:** list relevant definitions of terms and data items that are relevant to the domain being analyzed;
- **Document analysis:** review documents from within and outside of the organization to determine how the organization is currently operating, identify requirements or review possible solutions;
- **Interface analysis:** review how different parts of a solution connect and exchange information;
- **Metrics and key performance indicators:** determine how well solutions or the organization as a whole are performing;

■ **Non-functional requirements analysis:** determine the qualities a solution must have in order to be able to be used by the organization.

9.2   Other Techniques

Here are some key techniques that can be used to enhance your business analysis activities.

Pareto Analysis

Pareto analysis supports decision making by measuring the effect each input has on an outcome and then determining which course of action to take by addressing the inputs that have the greatest influence. Pareto analysis uses the Pareto principle that approximately 80% of the cause an outcome is usually due to 20% of its underlying inputs (for example 80% of an organization's helpdesk tickets come from 20% of their staff).

Pareto analysis focuses on delivering 'good enough' value by expending as little effort as possible[7]. Inputs are listed in descending order from the largest impact to the smallest impact and a strategy to address the inputs that make up 80% of the desired income or issue being analyzed is developed. See figure 9.2.

Tip: Using the Pareto principle and Pareto analysis keeps Business Analysts focused on working towards the most relevant outcomes for an organization and avoids spending an inordinate amount of time on details that, in the big picture, are not that relevant.

Value Stream Mapping

Value stream mapping is used to understand the factors that play into the development of a product or service. This technique was initially developed to assist in the improvement of manufacturing processes.

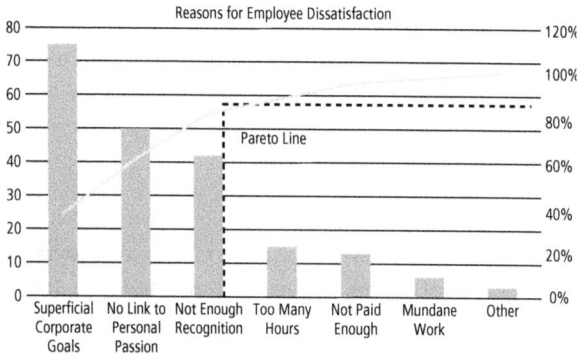

Figure 9.2 Pareto analysis example

In value stream mapping each step in the process is identified and the required inputs and outputs that trigger the step are documented. The amount of resources used vs. required in each step can also be included to identify opportunities for improvement. A future state diagram is developed to show how the process will work when it has been optimized[8]. See figure 9.3.

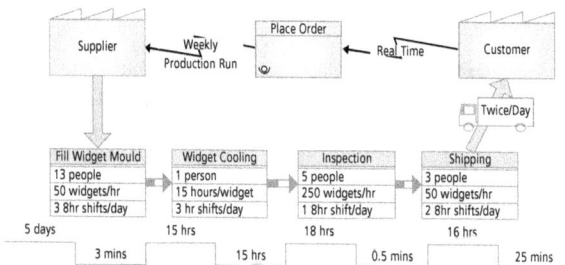

Figure 9.3 Sample value stream map

Value stream mapping enhances other process diagramming methods by including notations to track relevant measures that relate to the performance of the process. This allows teams or individuals to review the activities that occur at each step of the process and identify if there are ways that the step could be performed differently, or if there are times when the overall process is unnecessarily stalled or otherwise waiting for an input that could arrive sooner.

Success Factor Role Map

A success factor role map ties individual roles to the success factors of an organization[9]. This type of mapping supplements an organizational structure model and the roles and responsibilities matrices that describe what each individual role is expected to do. See figure 9.4.

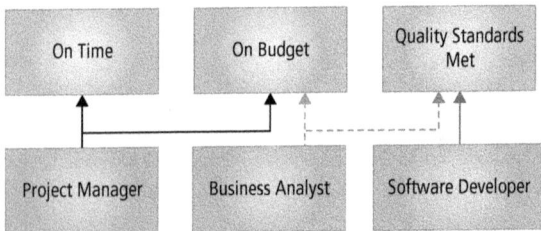

Figure 9.4 Success factor role map example

Success factor role maps can help with performing stakeholder analysis, confirming who needs to be engaged in an initiative, and defining and validating the future state structure of an organization.

Personal Planning Techniques

As noted in Chapter 8, personal organization is an important competency (competence) for Business Analysts. Personal planning techniques support this competency by providing a structured approach to determining what to work on, when, and for how long. The techniques include:

- **Getting Things Done[10]:** a personal organization method developed by David Allen. This approach involves continually capturing potential items that require action, setting aside time to process all potential items, defining and classifying actions so they can be addressed at the appropriate time, and periodically reviewing outstanding items to determine what is still relevant;
- **Personal backlog:** Scrum, an agile software development framework[11], uses a product backlog to track and prioritize all potential features the team could develop in a solution. A personal backlog uses the same general approach by listing all potential activities an individual must undertake and placing them in sequential priority. A context lens can be added to the backlog so that only items relevant to a particular situation (for example, being at a computer, in a meeting, etc.) are viewed when assessing what task to work on.

Further Reading on Additional Business Analysis Techniques

- *Business Analysis Techniques: 72 Essential Tools for Success* by James Cadle, Debra Paul and Paul Turner, British Informatics Society Ltd., 2010.
- *The Business Analyst's Handbook* by Howard Podeswa, Cengage Learning PTR., 2008.

10 Applying the *BABOK® Guide*

While the *BABOK® Guide* describes a collection of knowledge areas, tasks and their inter-relationships, it does not prescribe how, when and in what order to apply this information. There are many reasonable approaches that can be developed based on the specific initiative to be undertaken. How you decide to apply the *BABOK® Guide* depends on a variety of factors:

☑ What is the purpose of the initiative?

☑ How much time is there to be able to perform the work?

☑ Who is available to perform the business analysis tasks and what are their skills and experience?

☑ Which stakeholders will be involved in the initiative and what considerations need to be made to address their cultural and environmental norms?

☑ Are there any constraints on which activities and techniques are allowed to be applied?

Organizations often wish to develop a systematic approach to performing business analysis tasks in order to achieve predictable and consistent outcomes. This involves a combination of:

■ A methodology to ensure a similar approach is taken across all initiatives;

- Personal and organizational development models that assess current capabilities and can be used as a target for future growth;
- Continuous improvement techniques to support the implementation of changes in order to achieve the targets.

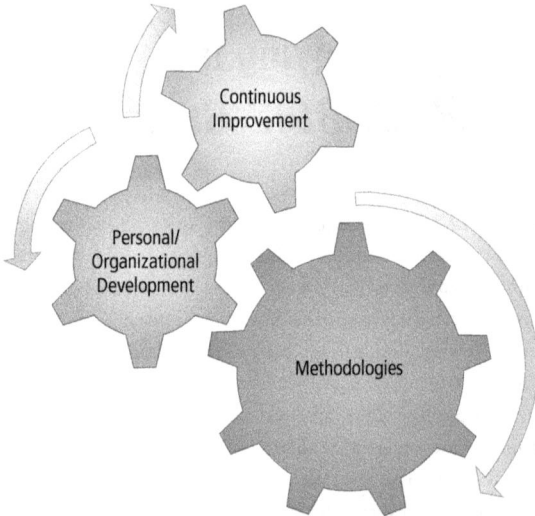

Figure 10.1 Systematic approach to performing business analysis tasks

This chapter discusses how these components create a system that enables organizations to tailor the *BABOK® Guide* information to their particular needs.

10.1 Developing a Business Analysis Methodology

A methodology is a formalized and repeatable approach that defines how to perform business analysis within a given context. Methodologies typically include:

☑ What tasks to perform and in what sequence;

☑ What deliverables are to be produced by which tasks;

☑ How deliverables are structured (usually in the form of templates);

☑ Rules governing how to apply the methodology to particular situations.

> ⚠️ **Example:** An organization has developed a methodology to address all business analysis situations it typically encounters. However, a business case only needs to be developed if the total cost of the project exceeds $500,000. Additionally, a traceability matrix between stakeholder and solution requirements is only needed when the requirements document will be published as part of an RFP.

To create a methodology for an organization, you need to identify similarities between the various initiatives the organization usually embarks upon, and identify what tasks can be standardized to achieve the desired outcomes.

10 Steps to Building a Methodology

1. **Identify the types of initiatives possible:** for instance, are they project-driven, embedded in the organization's regular operations, or a combination? A different methodology may be needed for each context, or the methodology may need to have different activities to address each context.

2. **Determine the scope of possible solution types:** if there is only one general type of possible solution (for example, an information technology solution, or construction of a physical product), then the methodology will likely have more specific deliverables and tasks that pertain to that type of solution. If the methodology must support many possible types of solutions (for example, process changes as well as new software packages), the deliverable templates will likely contain more generic descriptions or be separated for each type of solution.

3. **Define the role of business analysis in the initiative:** what exactly will be performed by one or more Business Analysts, and what will other roles be responsible for? Since the tasks described in the *BABOK® Guide* can overlap with other disciplines, the methodology should clearly define who will be performing what tasks, and who is ultimately responsible for each deliverable resulting from those tasks.

4. **Create the sequence of desired outcomes:** it is often easier to start with the desired final outcome (for example, a new solution is implemented), and work backwards to define what interim outcomes must happen in order to achieve the final outcome.

5. **Determine what deliverables support each outcome:** deliverables can take the form of a working solution, prototypes, documentation or other materials.

6. **Describe what tasks are needed to produce each deliverable:** these tasks should be assigned to specific roles within the methodology, if there are more roles than just the Business Analyst.

7. **Identify the sequence or dependencies between tasks:** you may also define phases within the methodology to show logical groupings of the tasks or important milestones between activities.

8. **Develop feedback loops that describe how deliverables are verified and validated:** this may include formal sign-off steps, review processes, mandatory traceability matrix deliverables, or other gating mechanisms.

9. **Decide how the methodology will adapt to change:** change can and will occur during the initiative, for example when new information is encountered that impacts outcomes, the external environment shifts, assumptions are determined to be false, or some other event occurs. The methodology should describe how changes will be assessed and acted upon when they are encountered.

10. **Document what happens to outputs once the initiative is completed:** for projects, how are the initiative's final deliverables transitioned to operations? If there are any loose ends (such as unmet requirements or outstanding issues), where are these documented and who is expected to address them?

> **Note:** No single methodology will work automatically in any context imaginable. However, organizations benefit from having a methodology when they perform initiatives on a regular basis that frequently require similar business analysis tasks.

An Example Methodology

The following graphic provides a high level overview of a simple business analysis methodology.

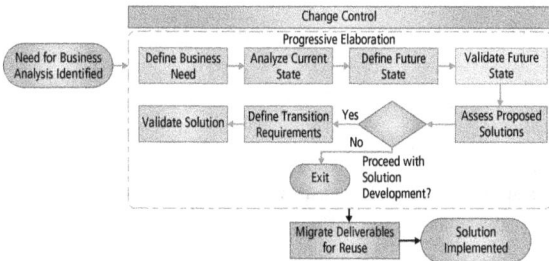

Figure 10.2 High level overview of a simple business analysis methodology

In this methodology, once a need for business analysis is identified, the Business Analysts assigned to the initiative proceed in an iterative fashion to progressively work towards a final solution to the problem. The activities depicted are performed in a sequential order but may be interrupted due to changes or new information introduced to the team.

Within each task the specific activities and deliverables involved
can be defined. In some cases certain techniques may be prescribed;
for example analyzing the current state may only be done through
document analysis and interviews.

Evaluating Your Methodology

Once a methodology is defined and implemented, it should be
evaluated to ensure it is delivering value to the organization. This
can entail a combination of qualitative and quantitative performance
measures, for example:

☑ Effort required to produce a deliverable;

☑ Number of cycles required to approve a deliverable;

☑ Variance between expected and actual time to complete activities
   and achieve milestones;

☑ Quality assessment of deliverables from their consumers (for
   example, the solution team, subject matter experts, and executives);

☑ Quality assessment from individuals involved in interactive
   business analysis activities (for example, workshops, interviews,
   and focus groups).

Tip: Ideally a newly-implemented methodology should be compared
against a baseline of performance measures for the same activities or
process prior to its implementation. If this is not possible, then the initial use
of the methodology can be used as a baseline for further assessment.

10.2 Business Analysis Maturity and Competency Models

Assessing how well individual Business Analysts perform their duties
and how the organization is performing overall are important if you
wish to improve future performance. A competency model assesses
how proficiently an individual can perform a task, while a maturity

model looks at how effective the organization performs an overall function.

Business Analyst Competency Model

The IIBA has developed a competency model[12] that contains 53 performance competencies and 20 underlying competencies. Each competency can be rated at one of the following five levels, which are based on the Dreyfus model of skill acquisition:

- **Novice:** the individual has a textbook understanding with no practical experience. As a result the novice typically adheres to defined rules and requires close supervision:
- **Advanced beginner:** the individual can do simple tasks independently, but will likely require supervision for more complex tasks:
- **Competent:** the individual can perform tasks without close supervision, and in general execute defined processes effectively:
- **Proficient:** the individual can not only perform nearly all tasks with minimal supervision, but can also supervise or guide others on the same tasks:
- **Expert:** the individual leverages a deep understanding of the task at hand. The expert can develop high quality results and also adapt to unforeseen circumstances or unique challenges in most situations.

The competency model provides a list of indicators for each competency to assist with determining how well an individual is performing the tasks described in the competency. The model also maps specific competency levels to job descriptions for Business Analysts at various levels of seniority.

> 💡 **Tip:** The IIBA's competency model is a good starting point to determine how to assess Business Analyst performance. However, not all competencies will be relevant to a specific organization, nor is it practical to measure all the competencies. Focus on the key competencies that have a strong correlation to the desired outcomes of your business analysis activities.

Business Analysis Maturity Models

There are multiple business analysis maturity models that have been developed, mainly by private companies as part of their business analysis service offerings. These models evaluate how consistently business analysis processes are able to be executed, and if there are mechanisms in place to evaluate and improve upon these processes over time. Generally these maturity models are based on the Capability Maturity Model Integration (CMMI) structure initially developed at Carnegie Mellon University, which defines five maturity levels[13]:

- **Initial:** processes are performed on an ad-hoc basis. There is minimal consistency between individuals who perform the processes and quality can vary greatly with each execution;
- **Managed:** processes are planned and executed in accordance with organizational policies. The processes are usually described so that there is a clear understanding of the purpose and expected result of the process;
- **Defined:** processes are described in detail through a combination of standards, procedures, tools and methods. Process execution with different individuals or in different situations yields relatively consistent results;
- **Quantitatively managed:** processes are defined and performance measures have been identified and are being collected for statistical analysis;

■ **Optimizing:** a continual improvement approach that uses
   the performance measures and root cause analysis to enable
   incremental increases in effective delivery over time.

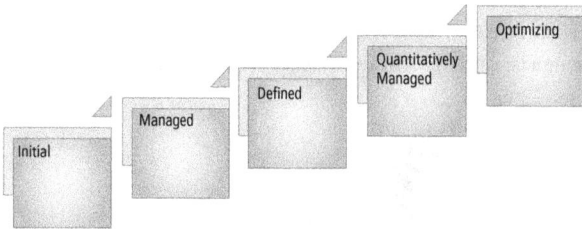

Figure 10.3 The five maturity levels of CMMI

A maturity model based on these levels or something similar may
be used to characterize the organization's business analysis practice
as a whole or for specific components (for example, requirements
management or solution validation).

> **Note:** A business analysis maturity model allows the organization to
> understand how strong its overall business analysis practices are and
> can be used to set targets for future improvement.

10.3 Improving Business Analysis Practices

With a methodology in place and measures to assess how well
individual Business Analysts and the overall business analysis team
are performing, targets can be set and plans can be put in place to
improve your business analysis practices.

> **Tip:** Don't try to improve in all areas at once. Start with key areas that
> will benefit the most from improvement, then determine when to collect
> information again and re-evaluate.

The Plan-Do-Check-Act cycle (otherwise known at the Deming Cycle) can be used to iteratively execute changes and evaluate their effectiveness in order to determine if the desired outcome is being achieved. This allows Business Analysts to see whether new approaches or changes to their methodology actually create value, and can provide insight into future adaptations to deliver additional positive results. See figure 10.4.

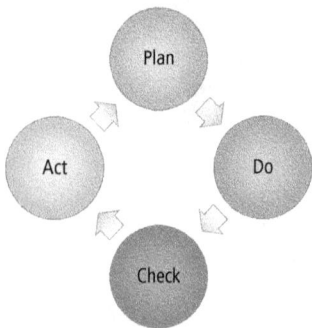

Figure 10.4 Plan-Do-Check-Act mechanism to Facilitate improvements

There are a variety of mechanisms that can be used to help with the design and implementation of improvements to business analysis practices:

- **Management-driven:** Business Analyst managers (be they in operational or project-based roles), in conjunction with Human Resource staff, work together to design individual and team evaluation criteria and targets to support practice improvements.
- **Consultant-driven:** external firms with expertise in business analysis practice improvement come in to provide insight into current practices and identify opportunities for improvement. Depending on the nature of their engagement, the consultants may only develop recommendations or they may also continue to be involved in their implementation.

- **Centre of Excellence:** while there is no universal definition, a Business Analysis Centre of Excellence (or BA CoE), is usually a formally recognized group within an organization that supports the development and improvement of business analysis practices[14,15]. In some organizations the BA CoE has a similar role to a Project Management Office that oversees all projects within the organization. In others the centre may define specific objectives and measures for Business Analysts, and set up structured sessions to develop standards and identify best practices within the organization.

- **Community of practice:** again there is no universal definition for what constitutes a community of practice. Generally communities of practice are viewed as less formal entities within an organization, and may have grown organically when a collection of Business Analysts decided they wanted to have a venue to discuss how they do their work and learn from each other[16]. Communities of practice may put in place similar objectives and develop similar outputs as a Centre of Excellence.

- **Extra-organizational entities and events:** entities such as IIBA, websites dedicated to sharing information on business analysis practices, and conferences with business analysis content are all places where individuals and teams can gain insights into ways to help improve their business analysis practice.

Note: Improvement techniques such as lessons learned, benchmarking and root cause analysis can be used during the Check and Act stages of the Deming Cycle to assist with evaluating how to improve your business analysis practices. Value stream mapping (described in Chapter 9) can be used to identify activities that could be changed or removed to improve effectiveness.

Appendix A Glossary

Unless otherwise specified, these definitions come from the Business Analysis Body of Knowledge® Version 2.0.

Assumption: influencing factors that are believed to be true but have not been confirmed to be accurate.

Business Analysis: the set of tasks and techniques used to work as a liaison among stakeholders in order to understand the structure, policies and operations of an organization, and recommend solutions that enable the organization to achieve its goals.

Business Analyst: a practitioner of business analysis.

Business Requirement: a higher level business rationale that, when addressed, will permit the organization to increase revenue, avoid costs, improve service, or meet regulatory requirements.

Change Management (information technology context): the process responsible for controlling the lifecycle of all changes, enabling beneficial changes to be made with minimum disruption to IT services[17].

Change Management (organizational context): the set of processes, tools and practices that are used to manage the people side of a change[18].

Competency: the knowledge, skills, abilities and behaviors that employees use in performing their work[19].

Component: a part or element of a larger whole[20].

Constraint: any limitations imposed on the solution that do not support the business or stakeholder needs.

Domain: the problem area undergoing analysis.

Deliverable: a deficiency in a product or service that reduces its quality or varies from a desired attribute, state, or functionality. See also requirements defect.

Elicitation: an activity within requirements development that identifies sources for requirements and then uses elicitation techniques (e.g., interviews, prototypes, facilitated workshops, documentation studies) to gather requirements from those sources.

Functional Requirement: a behavior, capability, or thing the solution must do for its stakeholders.

Goal: a state or condition the business must satisfy to reach its vision.

Initiative: any effort undertaken with a defined goal or objective.

Methodology: a set of processes, rules, templates, and working methods that prescribe how business analysis, solution development and implementation is performed in a particular context.

Model: a representation and simplification of reality developed to convey information to a specific audience to support analysis, communication and understanding.

Non-Functional Requirement: an environmental condition under which the solution must remain effective, or qualities the solution must have.

Objective: a target or metric that a person or organization seeks to meet in order to progress towards a goal.

Operations (Ongoing Operations): the ongoing activities of an organization performed to maintain and grow the organization that have no defined end date[21].

Organization: an autonomous unit within an enterprise under the management of a single individual or board, with a clearly defined boundary that works towards common goals and objectives. Organizations operate on a continuous basis, as opposed to an organizational unit or project team, which may be disbanded once its objectives are achieved.

Performance Measure: a quantifiable expression of the amount, cost, or result of activities that indicate how much, how well, and at what level, products or services are provided to customers during a given time period[22].

Process: a set of defined ad-hoc or sequenced collaborative activities performed in a repeatable fashion by an organization. Processes are triggered by events and may have multiple possible outcomes. A successful outcome of a process will deliver value to one or more stakeholders.

Project: a temporary endeavor undertaken to create a unique product, service or result.

Requirement:
1. A condition or capability needed by a stakeholder to solve a problem or achieve an objective;
2. A condition or capability that must be met or possessed by a solution or solution component to satisfy a contract, standard, specification or other formally imposed documents; or
3. A documented representation of a condition or capability as in 1. or 2.

Requirement State: a description of the mode or condition of being for a requirement. (Based on definition of state[23].)

Solution: a means to meet a business need by resolving a problem or allowing an organization to take advantage of an opportunity.

Solution Requirement: a characteristic of a solution that meets the business and stakeholder requirements. May be subdivided into functional and non-functional requirements.

Stakeholder: a group or person who has interests that may be affected by an initiative or influence over it.

Stakeholder Requirement: a statement of the needs of a particular stakeholder or class of stake- holders. They describe the needs that a given stakeholder has and how that stakeholder will interact with a solution. Stakeholder requirements serve as a bridge between business requirements and the various categories of solution requirements.

Subject Matter Expert (SME): a stakeholder with specific expertise in an aspect of the problem domain or potential solution alternatives or components.

Task: a piece of work to be done or undertaken[24].

Transition Requirement: describes a capability the solution must have in order to facilitate transition from the current state of the enterprise to the desired future state, but that will not be needed once that transition is complete.

Appendix B References

1. IIBA (2009). *A Guide to the Business Analysis Body of Knowledge (BABOK® guide), Version 2.0*. Toronto, ON: International Institute of Business Analysis.
2. History of IIBA. *International Institute of Business Analysis*. Retrieved June 15, 2013, from http://www.iiba.org/IIBA/About_IIBA/Governance/History_of_IIBA/IIBA_Website/About_IIBA/Governance_pages/History_of_IIBA.aspx?hkey=7f36c8c0-28da-468b-b9da-bc4e1077d69f.
3. Mintzberg, H. (1994). *The Fall and Rise of Strategic Planning*. In: *Harvard Business Review*, 72(1), p. 108-113.
4. Liedtka, J. (1998). *Strategic Thinking: Can it be Taught?* In: *Long Range Planning*. 1(1), p. 120-129.
5. Engaging [Def. 1]. (n.d.). In *Collins Online*, Retrieved June 30, 2013, from http://www.collinsdictionary.com/dictionary/english/engaging.
6. PMI, *What is Project Management?* Retrieved May 19, 2013 from http://www.pmi.org/About-Us/About-Us-What-is-Project-Management.aspx.
7. Pareto Analysis. *HCi*. Retrieved May 19, 2013 from http://www.hci.com.au/hcisite3/toolkit/paretos.htm.

8   Parker, J. (March 9, 2012). Business Analysis Techniques: Value
    Stream Mapping. *Enfocus Solutions.* Retrieved May 22, 2013 from
    http://blog.enfocussolutions.com/Powering_Requirements_
    Success/bid/128758/Business-Analysis-Techniques-Value-Stream-
    Mapping.

9   Accountability Framework System – Role Map. *Optimus|SBR.*
    Retrieved May 21, 2013 from http://optimussbr.com/services/
    strategy/accountability-framework-system/role-map.

10 About GTD. *David Allen Company.* Retrieved May 19, 2013 from
    http://www.davidco.com/about-gtd.

11 Core Scrum – Artifacts and Activities. *Scrum Alliance.* Retrieved
    July 15, 2013 from http://www.scrumalliance.org/why-scrum/core-
    scrum-artifacts-activities.

12 Business Analysis Competency Model Version 3. *International
    Institute of Business Analysis.* Retrieved on May 2, 2013 from
    http://www.iiba.org/IIBA/Professional_Development/Business_
    Analysis_Competency_Model/IIBA_Website/Professional_
    Development/CM_pages/CM.aspx?hkey=f07d564b-e5fc-418c-
    86c5-3c4c9de85501.

13 CMMI Product Team. (November 2010). *CMMI for Development,
    Version 1.3.* Retrieved from http://cmmiinstitute.com/assets/
    reports/10tr033.pdf.

14 Craig, W., Fisher, M., Garcia, S., Kaylor, C., Porter, J., & Reed, S.
    (December 2009). *Generalized Criteria and Evaluation Method for
    Center of Excellence: A Preliminary Report.* Retrieved from http://
    repository.cmu.edu/cgi/viewcontent.cgi?article=1287&context=sei.

15 Centre of Excellence [Def. 1]. In *Cambridge Dictionaries Online,*
    Retrieved May 2, 2013 from http://dictionary.cambridge.org/
    dictionary/business-english/centre-of-excellence.

16 Loxton, M. (June 1, 2011). *CoP vs CoE – What's the Difference and Why Should You Care?* Retrieved from http://mloxton.wordpress.com/2011/06/01/cop-vs-coe-%E2%80%93-what%E2%80%99s-the-difference-and-why-should-you-care/.

17 ITIL. (2011). *ITIL Glossary and Abbreviations.* Retrieved from http://www.itil-officialsite.com/nmsruntime/saveasdialog.aspx?lid=1180&.

18 Prosci Project Change Triangle. *Prosci.* Retrieved July 2, 2013 from http://www.change-management.com/tutorial-change-triangle-mod2.htm.

19 Competencies. (December 2, 2011). Treasury Board of Canada Secretariat. Retrieved July 3, 2013 from http://www.tbs-sct.gc.ca/tal/comp-eng.asp.

20 Component [Def. 1.]. In *Oxford Dictionaries Online,* Retrieved July 2, 2013 from http://oxforddictionaries.com/definition/english/component.

21 Verzuh, E. (2008). *The Fast Forward MBA in Project Management, Third Edition.* Hoboken, NJ: John Wiley & Sons, Inc.

22 Office of Financial Management, State of Washington. (August 2009). *Performance Measure Guide.* Retrieved from http://www.ofm.wa.gov/budget/instructions/other/2009performancemeasureguide.pdf.

23 State [Def. 1.]. In *Merriam-Webster Online,* Retrieved July 2, 2013 from http://www.merriam-webster.com/dictionary/state.

24 Task [Def. 1.]. In *Oxford Dictionaries Online,* Retrieved July 2, 2013 from http://oxforddictionaries.com/definition/english/task.

Business Information Management: BiSL®

BiSL® - A Framework for Business Information Management

This book describes a process framework for business information management: the Business Information Services Library (BiSL) – a public domain standard that is consistent with the IT Infrastructure Library (ITIL) and Application Services Library (ASL).

ISBN HARD COPY **978 90 8753 702 9**
ISBN EBOOK **978 90 8753 877 4**

BiSL®

English
€39.95
excl tax

BiSL® - Pocket Guide – 2nd Edition

This book describes the BiSL® framework, encompassing the best way to manage and execute business information management in day-to-day practice, and explaining how BiSL can help.

ISBN HARD COPY **978 90 8753 711 1**
ISBN EBOOK **978 90 8753 812 5**

BiSL®

English
€15.95
excl tax

www.ingramcontent.com/pod-product-compliance
Lightning Source LLC
Chambersburg PA
CBHW070407200326
41518CB00011B/2106